Implementation of the European Social Charter
Survey by country – 2001

Information document of the Secretariat
of the European Social Charter

French edition:

Application de la Charte sociale européenne. Aperçu par pays – 2001

ISBN 92-871-4715-9

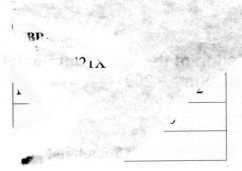

Council of Europe Publishing
F-67075 Strasbourg Cedex

ISBN 92-871-4716-7
© Council of Europe, January 2002
Printed at the Council of Europe

Table of Contents

III. Overview of the situation by country....................47

General overview of national situations....................134

Preface

The European Social Charter celebrates its fortieth anniversary on 18 October 2001. The Charter is a benchmark in the field of fundamental social rights, and its ratification has become one of the conditions for accession to the Council of Europe. Thanks to a major political effort by the Council's member states – culminating in the entry into force of the revised version in 1999 – the Charter now stands as a worthy complement to the European Convention on Human Rights.

For over thirty years, the European Committee of Social Rights has been seeking to clarify and give practical expression to the fundamental social rights enshrined in the Charter. Every year, it examines legislation and practice in most European countries and decides whether they are compatible with the commitments undertaken. Thus backed by an extensive and well-established body of case-law, the fundamental social rights guaranteed by the Charter are available and comprehensible to all – ordinary citizens, experts, judges, ombudsmen, NGOs, trade unions, members of parliament, etc.

This publication outlines the various improvements in Europeans' rights and quality of life that are directly or indirectly due to the decisions made by the European Committee of Social Rights, highlighting areas where the European Social Charter is working to good effect. It also indicates those aspects of national law and practice where progress is expected.

I. European Social Charter

A. GENERAL PRESENTATION

The European Social Charter, which was opened for signature in Turin in 1961 and entered into force in 1965, is a treaty guaranteeing Human Rights and fundamental freedoms in the economic and social spheres. The Charter complements the European Convention on Human Rights.

Three Protocols to the Charter have been adopted:

Protocol No. 1 (1988)
which adds new rights

Protocol No. 2 (1991)
which reforms the control mechanism based on reports

Protocol No. 3 (1995)
which provides for a procedure of collective complaints

Following a complete revision, the Charter of 1961 is gradually being replaced by the revised European Social Charter which was adopted in 1996 and entered into force in 1999.

B. SIGNATURES AND RATIFICATIONS
Signatures and ratifications of the Charter, its Protocols and the revised Charter, Situation at 1st December 2001

Member States	European Social Charter 1961		Additional Protocol 1988		Amending Protocol 1991		Collective Complaints Protocol 1995		Revised European Social Charter 1996	
	Signature	Ratification	Signature	Ratification	Signature	Ratification	Signature	Ratification	Signature	Ratification
Albania	(1)	–	(1)	–	(1)	–	(1)	–	21/09/98	–
Andorra	(1)	–	(1)	–	(1)	–	(1)	–	04/11/00	–
Armenia	–	–	–	–	–	–	–	–	18/10/01	–
Austria	22/07/63	29/10/69	04/12/90	–	07/05/92	13/07/95	07/05/99	–	07/05/99	–
Azerbaïjan	–	–	–	–	–	–	–	–	18/10/01	–
Belgium	18/10/61	16/10/90	20/05/92	–	22/10/91	21/09/00	14/05/96	–	03/05/96	–
Bulgaria	(2)	(2)	(3)	(3)	(2)	(2)	(4)	(4)	21/09/98	07/06/00
Croatia	08/03/99	–	08/03/99	–	08/03/99	–	08/03/99	–	–	–
Cyprus	22/05/67	07/03/68	05/05/88	(3)	21/10/91	01/06/93	09/11/95	06/08/96	03/05/96	27/09/00
Czech Republic	27/05/92*	03/11/99	27/05/92*	17/11/99	27/05/92*	17/11/99	–	–	04/11/00	–
Denmark	18/10/61	03/03/65	27/08/96	27/08/96	–	**	09/11/95	–	03/05/96	–
Estonia	(2)	(2)	(3)	(3)	(2)	(2)	(2)	–	04/05/98	11/09/00
Finland	09/02/90	29/04/91	09/02/90	29/04/91	16/03/92	18/08/94	09/11/95	17/07/98	03/05/96	–
France	18/10/61	09/03/73	22/06/89	(2)	21/10/91	24/05/95	09/11/95	07/05/99	03/05/96	07/05/99
Georgia	(1)	–	(1)	–	(1)	–	(1)	–	30/06/00	–
Germany	18/10/61	27/01/65	05/05/88	–	–	**	–	–	–	–
Greece	18/10/61	06/06/84	05/05/88	18/06/98	29/11/91	12/09/96	18/06/98	18/06/98	03/05/96	–

Hungary	13/12/91	08/07/99	—	—	13/12/91	**	—	—	—	—
Iceland	15/01/76	15/01/76	05/05/88	—	—	**	—	—	04/11/98	—
Ireland	18/10/61	07/10/64	(3)	(3)	14/05/97	14/05/97	04/11/00	04/11/00	04/11/00	04/11/00
Italy	18/10/61	22/10/65	05/05/88	26/05/94	21/10/91	27/01/95	09/11/95	03/11/97	03/05/96	05/07/99
Latvia	29/05/97	—	29/05/97	—	29/05/97	—	—	—	—	—
Liechtenstein	09/10/91	—		—	—	—	—	—	—	—
Lithuania	(2)	(2)	(3)	(3)	(2)	(2)	(2)	—	08/09/97	29/06/01
Luxembourg	18/10/61	10/10/91	05/05/88	—	21/10/91	**	—	—	11/02/98	—
Malta	26/05/88	04/10/88	—	—	21/10/91	16/02/94	—	—	—	—
Moldova	(1)	—	(1)	(1)	(1)	—	(1)	—	03/11/98	08/11/01
Netherlands	18/10/61	22/04/80	14/06/90	05/08/92	21/10/91	01/06/93	—	—	07/05/01	—
Norway	18/10/61	26/10/62	10/12/93	10/12/93	21/10/91	21/10/91	20/03/97	20/03/97	07/05/01	07/05/01
Poland	26/11/91	25/06/97	—	—	18/04/97	25/06/97	—	—	—	—
Portugal	01/06/82	30/09/91	(1)	—	24/02/92	08/03/93	09/11/95	20/03/98	03/05/96	—
Romania	04/10/94	(2)	(3)	(3)	(2)	(2)	(2)	—	14/05/97	07/05/99
Russia	(1)	—	(1)	—	(1)	—	(1)	—	14/09/00	—
San Marino	—	—	—	—	—	—	—	—	18/10/01	—
Slovakia	27/05/92*	22/06/98	27/05/92*	22/06/98	27/05/92*	22/06/98	18/11/99	—	18/11/99	—
Slovenia	11/10/97	(2)	11/10/97	(3)	11/10/97	(2)	11/10/97	(4)	11/10/97	07/05/99
Spain	27/04/78	06/05/80	05/05/88	24/01/00	21/10/91	24/01/00	—	—	23/10/00	—
Sweden	18/10/61	17/12/62	05/05/88	05/05/89	21/10/91	18/03/92	09/11/95	29/05/98	03/05/96	29/05/98
Switzerland	06/05/76	—	—	—	—	—	—	—	—	—

Member States	European Social Charter 1961		Additional Protocol 1988		Amending Protocol 1991		Collective Complaints Protocol 1995		Revised European Social Charter 1996	
	Signature	*Ratification*	*Signature*	*Ratification*	*Signature*	*Ratification*	*Signature*	*Ratification*	*Signature*	*Ratification*
"The Former Yugoslav Republic of Macedonia"	05/05/98	–	05/05/98	–	05/05/98	–	–	–	–	–
Turkey	18/10/61	24/11/89	05/05/98	–	–	**	–	–	–	–
Ukraine	02/05/96	–	(1)	–	(1)	–	(1)	–	07/05/99	–
The United Kingdom	18/10/61	11/07/62	–	–	21/10/91	**	–	–	07/11/97	–

*   Date of signature by the Czech and Slovak Federal Republic.

**   State whose ratification is necessary for the entry into force of the Protocol.

(1)   State having signed the revised Social Charter.

(2)   State having ratified the revised Social Charter.

(3)   State having accepted the rights (or certain of the rights) guaranteed by the Protocol by ratifying the revised Charter.

(4)   State having accepted the collective complaints procedure by a declaration made in application of Article D para. 2 of Part IV of the revised Social Charter.

C. RIGHTS GUARANTEED[1]

The following list enumerates the rights of the revised Charter.

1. Health

Right to health (Article 11)
    right of access to health (§1)
    right to health prevention : education and consultation (§2)
    right to health prevention : regulations and prophylactic measures (§3)

Right to health and safety at work
    general policy (Article 3§1), regulations (Article 3§2), supervision (Article 3§3), occupational health services (Article 3§4)
    right to compensatory time off in dangerous occupations (Article 2§4)

Rights of children (Article 7)
    prohibition of employment of children under 15 (§§1 and 3)
    prohibition of dangerous work for young people under 18 (§2)
    right of young people between 15 and 18 to special working conditions: working time (§4), holiday with pay (§7), night work (§8), medical control (§9)

Rights related to maternity (Article 8)
    right to maternity leave and benefits (§1)
    right to time off for nursing (§3)
    regulation of night work(§4)
    prohibition of employment in certain dangerous work (§5)

2. Housing

Right to housing (Article 31)
Rights of family (housing) (Article 16)

3. Employment/Right to organise

Right to work (Article 1)
    policy aimed at full employment (§1)
    right to free employment services (§3)
    right to vocational guidance, training and rehabilitation (§4)

---

[1] When ratifying the Charter or the revised Charter, states have the possibility of selecting those provisions by which they accept to be bound, on condition, however, of accepting a minimum number of provisions. The tables below 'D. Acceptance) show the provisions accepted state-by-state.

prohibition of discrimination in employment (§2)
prohibition of forced labour (§2)

Equality between women and men
See Equality

Right of disabled persons to special measures concerning access to work and working conditions (Article 15§2)

Right to decent conditions of employment (Articles 1, 2 et 4)

right to dignity at work (Article 26)

right to reasonable working time (Article 2§1)
right to public holidays with pay (Article 2§2)
right to annual holiday with pay (Article 2§3)
right to weekly rest (Article 2§4)
right to special guarantees in case f night work (Article 2§6)

right to a fair remuneration (Article 4§1)
right of young people between 15 and 18 to special working conditions (wage) (Article 7§5),
right to increased remuneration for overtime (Article 4§2)
right to protection of claim in the event of the insolvency of the employer (Article 25)
right to guarantees in case of deduction from wages (Article 4§5)

right to protection in case of dismissal (Articles 4§4 and 24)
prohibition of dismissal during maternity leave (Article 8§2)

Information and consultation of workers
right of the employee to information concerning essential aspects of the employment relationship (Article 2§6)
right to information and consultation (Article 21)
right to take part in the determination and improvement of the working conditions (Article 22)

Right to organise
right to organise (Article 5)
right to collective bargaining (Article 6): joint consultation (§1), machinery for voluntary negotiations (§2), conciliation and arbitration (§3), strikes and lock-outs (§4)
right to information and consultation (Article 21)
right to take part in the determination and improvement of the working conditions (Article 22)

right to information and consultation of workers representatives in collective redundancy procedures (Article 29)
right of workers' representatives to special guarantees (Article 28)

4. Education

Rights of children (Article 7)
prohibition of children employment under 15 (§§1 and 3)
right of young people between 15 and 18 to special working conditions: working time (§4), time for training (§7), holiday with pay (§7), night work (§8)

Right to vocational guidance (Article 9)

Right to vocational training (Article 10)
right to access to higher education (§1), to apprenticeship (§2) to continuing training and retraining (§3), measures facilitating access (§5)
right of long term unemployed persons to special reintegration measures (§4)

Right of disabled people to vocational guidance and training (Article 15§1)

Rights of young persons (free education) (Article 17§2)

5. Social protection

Right to social security (Article 12)
existence and maintenance of a social security system (§1)
minimum level (§2)
improvement and safeguard (§3)

Rights related to maternity (Article 8)
right to maternity leave and benefits (§1)
Right of elderly to social protection (Article 24)
Rights of family (legal protection, family benefits, adequate family policy) (Article 16)

Right to protection against poverty and social exclusion (Article 30)
Right to social and medical assistance (Article 13)
individual right to adequate social and medical assistance (§1)
right to advice and to social services (§3)

Right to social services (Article 14)

Right of disabled people to social integration and participation (Article 15§3)

Rights of young persons (legal and social protection) (Article 17§1)

6. Movement of persons

Rights related to the entry into the territory
> right to simplification and liberalisation of formalities related to immigration (Article 18§§1 to 3)
> right to services of assistance and information relating to migration (Article 19§1)
> right to assistance for departure, journey and reception (Article 19§2)
> right to co-operation between social services (Article 19§3)
> right to family reunion (Article 19§6)

Rights of resident migrants
> right to equal treatment : see Equality
> transfer of earnings and savings (Article 19§9), teaching of the language of the receiving state (Article 19§11), teaching of the mother tongue (Article 19§12)

Rights related to leaving the territory
> right to emergency assistance until repatriation has taken place (Article 13§4)
> right of nationals to leave the country (Article 18§4)
> right to guarantees in case of expulsion or repatriation (Articles 13§§1/4 and 19§8)

7. Equality

Nationality (of a Contracting State)
> Appendix to the Charter
> vocational guidance, training and rehabilitation (Articles 1§4 and 10§5)
> social security and social and medical assistance (Articles 12§4 and 13§1)
> conditions of employment, housing and right to organise (Article 19§4)
> taxes and dues (Article 19§5)
> legal proceedings (Article 19§7)

Health
> general non-discrimination clause (Article E)
> vocational guidance, training and rehabilitation (Article 1§4)

Property
> general non-discrimination clause (Article E)
> non-discrimination in respect of social and political rights (Article 13§2)

Sex

general non-discrimination clause (Article E)

right to equal treatment and opportunities in employment (Articles 1§2 and 20)

right to equal pay (Article 4§3)

right of workers with family responsibilities to equal opportunities and equal treatment (Article 27)

Birth

general non-discrimination clause (Article E)

rights of young persons (legal and social protection) (Article 17§1)

Trade union membership

general non-discrimination clause (Article E)

right to organise (Article 5)

Other grounds

general non-discrimination clause (Article E)

prohibition of discrimination in employment (Article 1§2)

D. ACCEPTANCE
Accepted provisions of the European Social Charter (1961)

Legend: ▨ Accepted   ☐ Not accepted

Provision of the Charter	Austria	Belgium	Czech Rep.	Denmark	Finland	Germany	Greece	Hungary	Iceland	Luxembourg	Malta	Netherlands*	Poland	Portugal	Slovakia	Spain	Turkey	United Kingdom
Article 1 (1)																		
Article 1 (2)																		
Article 1 (3)																		
Article 1 (4)																		
Article 2 (1)																		
Article 2 (2)																		
Article 2 (3)																		
Article 2 (4)																		
Article 2 (5)																		
Article 3 (1)																		
Article 3 (2)																		
Article 3 (3)																		
Article 4 (1)																		
Article 4 (2)																		
Article 4 (3)																		

* As regards the Netherlands Antilles and Aruba, the Kingdom of the Netherlands has accepted Articles 1, 5, 6, 16 and Article 1 of the Additional Protocol.

Provision of the Charter	Austria	Belgium	Czech Rep.	Denmark	Finland	Germany	Greece	Hungary	Iceland	Luxembourg	Malta	Netherlands*	Poland	Portugal	Slovakia	Spain	Turkey	United Kingdom
Article 4 (4)		✓	✓				✓		✓		✓	✓	✓	✓	✓	✓		✓
Article 4 (5)	✓	✓	✓		✓	✓	✓		✓		✓	✓	✓	✓	✓	✓	✓	✓
Article 5	✓	✓	✓	✓	✓	✓		✓	✓	✓	✓	✓	✓	✓	✓	✓		✓
Article 6 (1)	✓	✓	✓	✓	✓	✓	✓	✓	✓	✓	✓	✓	✓	✓	✓	✓		✓
Article 6 (2)	✓	✓	✓	✓	✓	✓	✓	✓	✓	✓	✓	✓	✓	✓	✓	✓	✓	✓
Article 6 (3)	✓	✓	✓	✓	✓	✓	✓	✓	✓	✓	✓	✓	✓	✓	✓	✓	✓	✓
Article 6 (4)	✓	✓	✓	✓	✓	✓	✓	✓	✓	✓	✓		✓	✓	✓	✓	✓	✓
Article 7 (1)	✓	✓	✓		✓	✓	✓	✓	✓	✓	✓	✓		✓	✓	✓	✓	
Article 7 (2)	✓	✓	✓		✓	✓	✓	✓	✓	✓	✓	✓	✓	✓	✓	✓	✓	✓
Article 7 (3)	✓	✓	✓	✓	✓	✓	✓	✓	✓	✓	✓	✓	✓	✓	✓	✓	✓	✓
Article 7 (4)	✓	✓	✓	✓	✓	✓	✓	✓	✓	✓	✓	✓	✓	✓	✓	✓	✓	✓
Article 7 (5)	✓	✓	✓		✓	✓	✓	✓	✓	✓	✓	✓	✓	✓	✓	✓	✓	✓
Article 7 (6)	✓	✓	✓	✓	✓	✓	✓	✓	✓	✓	✓	✓	✓	✓	✓	✓	✓	
Article 7 (7)	✓	✓	✓		✓	✓	✓	✓	✓	✓	✓	✓	✓	✓	✓	✓		✓
Article 7 (8)	✓	✓	✓		✓	✓		✓	✓	✓	✓	✓	✓	✓	✓	✓	✓	✓
Article 7 (9)	✓	✓	✓		✓	✓		✓	✓	✓	✓	✓	✓	✓	✓	✓	✓	✓
Article 7 (10)	✓	✓	✓	✓	✓	✓	✓	✓	✓	✓	✓	✓	✓	✓	✓	✓		✓

* As regards the Netherlands Antilles and Aruba, the Kingdom of the Netherlands has accepted Articles 1, 5, 6, 16 and Article 1 of the Additional Protocol.

Provision of the Charter	Austria	Belgium	Czech Rep.	Denmark	Finland	Germany	Greece	Hungary	Iceland	Luxembourg	Malta	Netherlands*	Poland	Portugal	Slovakia	Spain	Turkey	United Kingdom
Article 8 (1)	●	●	●	●		●	●	●		●	●	●	●	●	●	●	●	●
Article 8 (2)	●	●	●	●		●	●	●		●	●	●	●	●	●	●		
Article 8 (3)	●	●	●	●		●	●	●		●	●	●	●	●	●	●		
Article 8 (4)	●	●	●				●	●		●		●	●	●	●	●[1]	●	●
Article 9	●	●				●	●	●	●	●	●	●	●	●	●	●	●	●
Article 10 (1)	●	●		●		●	●		●	●	●	●	●	●	●	●	●	●
Article 10 (2)	●	●		●		●	●			●	●	●	●	●	●	●	●	●
Article 10 (3)	●	●		●		●	●			●	●	●		●	●	●	●	●
Article 10 (4)	●	●		●		●	●		●	●	●[2]	●		●	●	●	●	●
Article 11 (1)	●	●	●	●	●	●	●	●		●	●	●	●	●	●	●	●	●
Article 11 (2)	●	●	●	●	●	●	●	●		●	●	●	●	●	●	●	●	●
Article 11 (3)	●	●	●	●	●	●	●	●		●	●	●	●	●	●	●	●	●
Article 12 (1)	●	●	●	●	●	●	●	●	●	●	●	●	●	●	●	●	●	
Article 12 (2)	●	●	●	●	●	●	●	●	●	●		●	●	●	●	●	●	
Article 12 (3)	●	●	●	●	●	●	●	●	●	●	●	●	●	●	●	●	●	●
Article 12 (4)	●	●	●	●	●	●	●	●		●		●	●	●	●	●	●	

[1] Spain has denounced sub-paragraph b with effect on 5 June 1991.

[2] Only the provisions of paragraph 4 a and d have been accepted.

* As regards the Netherlands Antilles and Aruba, the Kingdom of the Netherlands has accepted Articles 1, 5, 6, 16 and Article 1 of the Additional Protocol.

Provision of the Charter	Austria	Belgium	Czech Rep.	Denmark	Finland	Germany	Greece	Hungary	Iceland	Luxembourg	Malta	Netherlands*	Poland	Portugal	Slovakia	Spain	Turkey	United Kingdom
Article 13 (1)																		
Article 13 (2)																		
Article 13 (3)															☐			
Article 13 (4)																		
Article 14 (1)																		
Article 14 (2)																		
Article 15 (1)			☐					☐					☐				☐	
Article 15 (2)																		
Article 16																		
Article 17																		
Article 18 (1)			☐								☐		☐					
Article 18 (2)			☐															
Article 18 (3)	☐												☐		☐			
Article 18 (4)																		

* As regards the Netherlands Antilles and Aruba, the Kingdom of the Netherlands has accepted Articles 1, 5, 6, 16 and Article 1 of the Additional Protocol.

Provision of the Charter	Austria	Belgium	Czech Rep.	Denmark	Finland	Germany	Greece	Hungary	Iceland	Luxembourg	Malta	Netherlands*	Poland	Portugal	Slovakia	Spain	Turkey	United Kingdom
Article 19 (1)	■	■								■		■	■	■		■		■
Article 19 (2)		■				■				■		■	■	■		■		■
Article 19 (3)		■				■	■			■		■	■	■		■		■
Article 19 (4)	■	■				■	■			■		■	■	■		■		■
Article 19 (5)		■				■	■			■		■	■	■		■		■
Article 19 (6)		■				■	■			■		■	■	■		■		■
Article 19 (7)						■	■			■		■	■	■		■		■
Article 19 (8)		■				■	■			■		■	■	■		■		■
Article 19 (9)		■	■			■	■			■		■	■	■		■		■
Article 19 (10)										■		■	■	■		■		■

Accepted provisions of the Additional Protocol No. 1 (1988)

	Austria	Belgium	Czech Rep.	Denmark	Finland	Germany	Greece	Hungary	Iceland	Luxembourg	Malta	Netherlands*	Poland	Portugal	Slovakia	Spain	Turkey	United Kingdom
Article 1					■		■							■		■		
Article 2					■		■					■		■		■		
Article 3					■		■							■		■		
Article 4																■		

* As regards the Netherlands Antilles and Aruba, the Kingdom of the Netherlands has accepted Articles 1, 5, 6, 16 and Article 1 of the Additional Protocol.

3. Accepted provisions of the revised European Social Charter (1996)

Article of the Revised Charter	Bulgaria	Cyprus	Estonia	France	Ireland	Italy	Lithuania	Moldova	Norway	Romania	Slovenia	Sweden
Article 1 (1)	■	■	■	■	■	■	■	■	■	■	■	■
Article 1 (2)	■	■	■	■	■	■	■	■	■	■	■	■
Article 1 (3)	■	■	■	■	■	■	■	■	■	■	■	■
Article 1 (4)	■	■	■	■	■	■	■	■	■	■	■	
Article 2 (1)	■	■	■	■	■	■	■	■	■	■	■	
Article 2 (2)	■	■	■	■	■	■	■	■	■	■	■	■
Article 2 (3)				■	■	■	■	■	■		■	■
Article 2 (4)	■	■	■	■	■	■	■	■	■	■	■	■
Article 2 (5)	■	■	■	■	■	■	■	■	■	■	■	■
Article 2 (6)	■	■	■	■	■	■	■	■	■	■	■	■
Article 2 (7)	■			■	■	■	■	■		■	■	■
Article 3 (1)	■	■	■	■	■	■	■	■		■	■	■
Article 3 (2)	■	■	■	■	■	■	■	■	■	■	■	■
Article 3 (3)	■	■	■	■	■	■	■	■	■	■	■	■
Article 3 (4)	■	■	■	■	■	■	■	■	■	■	■	■
Article 4 (1)	■	■	■	■	■	■	■		■	■	■	■
Article 4 (2)	■	■	■	■	■	■	■		■	■	■	■
Article 4 (3)	■	■	■	■	■	■	■	■	■	■	■	■
Article 4 (4)	■	■	■	■	■	■	■	■	■	■	■	■
Article 4 (5)	■	■	■	■	■	■	■	■	■	■	■	

Article of the Revised Charter	Bulgaria	Cyprus	Estonia	France	Ireland	Italy	Lithuania	Moldova	Norway	Romania	Slovenia	Sweden
Article 5	■	■	■	■	■	■	■	■	■	■	■	■
Article 6 (1)	■	■	■	■	■	■	■	■	■	■	■	■
Article 6 (2)	■	■	■	■	■	■	■	■	■	■	■	■
Article 6 (3)	■	■	■	■	■	■	■	■	■	■	■	■
Article 6 (4)	■	■	■	■	■	■	■	■	■	■	■	■
Article 7 (1)	■	■	■	■	■	■	■	■	■	■	■	■
Article 7 (2)	■	■	■	■	■	■	■	■	■	■	■	■
Article 7 (3)	■	■	■	■	■	■	■	■	■	■	■	■
Article 7 (4)	■	■	■	■	■	■	■	■	■	■	■	■
Article 7 (5)	■	□	□	■	■	■	■	□	□	■	■	□
Article 7 (6)	■	□	■	■	■	■	■	■	□	■	■	■
Article 7 (7)	■	■	■	■	■	■	■	■	■	■	■	■
Article 7 (8)	■	□	■	■	■	■	■	■	□	■	■	□
Article 7 (9)	■	■	■	■	■	■	■	■	■	■	■	■
Article 7 (10)	■	■	■	■	■	■	■	■	■	■	■	■
Article 8 (1)	■	■	■	■	■	■	■	■	■	■	■	■
Article 8 (2)	■	■	■	■	■	■	■	■	■	■	■	■
Article 8 (3)	■	■	■	■	□	■	■	■	■	■	■	■
Article 8 (4)	■	■	■	■	■	■	■	■	■	■	■	■
Article 8 (5)	■	■	■	■	■	■	■	■	■	■	■	■

Article of the Revised Charter	Bulgaria	Cyprus	Estonia	France	Ireland	Italy	Lithuania	Moldova	Norway	Romania	Slovenia	Sweden
Article 9												
Article 10 (1)												
Article 10 (2)												
Article 10 (3)												
Article 10 (4)												
Article 10 (5)												
Article 11 (1)												
Article 11 (2)												
Article 11 (3)												
Article 12 (1)												
Article 12 (2)												
Article 12 (3)												
Article 12 (4)												
Article 13 (1)												
Article 13 (2)												
Article 13 (3)												
Article 13 (4)												
Article 14 (1)												
Article 14 (2)												

Article of the Revised Charter	Bulgaria	Cyprus	Estonia	France	Ireland	Italy	Lithuania	Moldova	Norway	Romania	Slovenia	Sweden
Article 15 (1)		X	X	X	X	X	X	X	X	X	X	X
Article 15 (2)		X	X	X	X	X	X	X	X		X	X
Article 15 (3)	X		X	X	X	X	X		X	X	X	X
Article 16	X		X	X	X	X	X	X	X		X	X
Article 17 (1)	X		X	X	X	X	X	X	X	X	X	X
Article 17 (2)	X		X	X	X	X	X		X	X	X	X
Article 18 (1)		X		X	X	X	X	X	X	X	X	X
Article 18 (2)		X		X	X	X	X	X	X	X		X
Article 18 (3)		X	X	X	X	X	X	X	X	X	X	X
Article 18 (4)	X	X	X	X	X	X	X	X	X	X	X	X
Article 19 (1)		X	X	X	X	X	X			X	X	X
Article 19 (2)		X	X	X	X	X	X	X	X	X	X	X
Article 19 (3)		X	X	X	X	X	X	X	X	X	X	X
Article 19 (4)		X	X	X	X	X	X	X	X	X	X	X
Article 19 (5)		X	X	X	X	X	X	X	X	X	X	X
Article 19 (6)		X	X	X	X	X	X	X	X	X	X	X
Article 19 (7)		X	X	X	X	X	X	X	X	X	X	X
Article 19 (8)			X	X	X	X	X	X	X	X	X	X
Article 19 (9)			X	X	X	X	X	X	X	X	X	X
Article 19 (10)			X	X	X	X	X	X		X	X	X
Article 19 (11)			X	X	X	X	X	X	X	X	X	X
Article 19 (12)			X	X	X	X	X	X	X	X	X	X

Article of the Revised Charter	Bulgaria	Cyprus	Estonia	France	Ireland	Italy	Lithuania	Moldova	Norway	Romania	Slovenia	Sweden
Article 20	X	X	X	X	X	X	X		X		X	X
Article 21	X		X	X	X	X	X		X		X	X
Article 22	X		X	X		X	X		X	X	X	X
Article 23		X	X	X	X	X		X	X	X	X	
Article 24	X	X	X	X	X	X	X	X			X	X
Article 25	X	X		X	X	X	X	X	X		X	X
Article 26 (1)	X		X	X	X	X		X			X	X
Article 26 (2)		X	X	X	X	X	X	X			X	X
Article 27 (1)			X	X	X	X	X	X			X	X
Article 27 (2)	X		X	X	X	X	X	X			X	X
Article 27 (3)	X	X	X	X	X	X	X	X			X	X
Article 28			X	X	X	X	X	X	X		X	X
Article 29			X	X	X	X	X	X	X		X	X
Article 30				X	X	X	X	X	X		X	X
Article 31 (1)				X	X	X			X		X	X
Article 31 (2)				X	X	X			X		X	X
Article 31 (3)				X	X	X			X		X	X

II. European Committee of Social Rights

> Compliance with the commitments set out in the Charter is subject to international supervision by an independent body – the European Committee of Social Rights.[1]

A. COMPOSITION

The European Committee of Social Rights is an independent supervisory body. It is made up of twelve independent experts[2] "of the highest integrity and of recognised competence in national and international social questions". The experts are elected by the Committee of Ministers.

They are elected for a term of 6 years and may be re-elected for one further term. They sit in an individual capacity and may not perform duties incompatible with the requirements of independence, impartiality and availability inherent in their office.

The Committee meets 8 times a year, each session lasts one week. In order to rationalise and speed up its work, the Committee has established two working groups which prepare the decisions.

On 9 September 1999, the Committee adopted new rules of procedure for its work within the framework of the two supervisory procedures (see below).

---

[1] This has been the name of the Committee since 1999.

[2] The 1961 Social Charter provided that the maximum number of experts was to be 7 (Article 25). Protocol No. 2 amended the Charter so as to provide that the European Committee of Social Rights was to be made up of at least 9 members and the Ministers' Deputies took a decision to this effect in March 1994. In order to increase legal competence within the Committee and to facilitate the integration of the legal experience of the new Contracting Parties, the Committee of Ministers decided in May 2001 that the Committee's membership would be increased from 9 to 12 and subsequently to 15.

As at 1ˢᵗ August 2001, the composition of the Committee was as follows (in order of precedence):

Mr Stein EVJU, <u>President</u>, Professor of Labour Law and Commercial Law, Norwegian School of Management, Sandvika (Norway)

M. Nikitas ALIPRANTIS, <u>Vice-President</u>, Professor, Democritos University of Thrace, Komotini (Greece)

Mr Matti MIKKOLA, <u>General rapporteur</u>, Professor of Labour Law, Department of Private Law, University of Helsinki (Finland) - Professor of Social Policy, University of Tartu (Estonia)

Mr Rolf BIRK, Professor of Labour Law, Director of the Institute of Labour Law and Industrial Relations in the European Community, University of Trier (Germany)

Mr Konrad GRILLBERGER, Professor, Director of the Institute of Labour Law and Social Legislation, University of Salzburg (Austria)

Mr Alfredo BRUTO DA COSTA, Assistant Professor, Portuguese Catholic University, Lisbon (Portugal)

Mᵐᵉ Micheline JAMOULLE, Professor, Law Faculty, University of Liège (Belgium)

M. Tekin AKILLIOĞLU, Professor of Public Law, Director of the Human Rights Centre, University of Ankara (Turkey)

M Jean-Michel BELORGEY, *Conseiller d'Etat*, Head of the International Co-operation Unit, Reports and Studies' Section, *Conseil d'Etat*, Paris (France)

Mrs Csilla KOLLONAY LEHOCZKY, Professor, Legal Studies Department, Central European University, Budapest (Hungary)

Ms Polonca KONCAR, Professor, Law Faculty, University of Ljubljana (Slovenia)

Mr Gerard QUINN, Professor, Law Faculty, National University of Ireland at Galway (Ireland)

B. PROCEDURES

1. Procedure of control regarding reports

ASSESSMENT INFORMATION

States shall on a regular basis submit reports concerning their application of the Charter.

The States present an annual report on how they apply the Charter, in law and in practice. Each report pertains to a part of the accepted provisions: in odd years the report concerns the 'hard core' provisions[1], in even years half of the other provisions, i.e. a report on the hard core provisions every two years and a report on the provisions not forming part of the hard core every four years. The Committee of Ministers has laid down a precise calendar for the presentation of reports (see C. Deadlines).

A form, adopted by the Committee of Ministers, lists the information that has to be contained in the reports for assessing whether States are complying with the Charter.[2]

When a State ratifies the Charter, it has to submit an initial report on all of the Charter provisions which it accepts. A second report, also covering all the accepted provisions, has to be submitted two years after the submission of the first. Thereafter, only partial reports are required. States ratifying the revised Charter come directly under the partial report system.

The reports are public as soon as they reach the Council of Europe and may be consulted on the Internet.[3]

---

[1] The hard core provisions of the Charter are: the right to work (Article 1), the right to organise and the right to bargain collectively (Articles 5 and 6), the right to social security (Article 12), the right to assistance (Article 13), rights of the family (Article 16) and migrants' rights (Article 19). The hard core of the revised Charter additionally includes children's rights (Article 7) and the right to equal opportunities and equal treatment between men and women in employment (Article 20).

[2] The latest version of the form for the Charter dates from September 1999. The form for the revised Charter was adopted in January 2001.

[3] www.esc.coe.int

The States are under a further obligation to forward a copy of their reports to national employers' associations and trade unions,[1] which may make comments on the reports and send those comments directly to the Committee. Furthermore, the Secretariat sends copies of the reports to non-governmental organisations which have consultative status with the Council of Europe and have particular competence in matters governed by the Social Charter.[2]

If the European Committee of Social Rights takes the view that it does not have sufficient information to make a finding, it may either contact the governments directly by letter or organise meetings[3] with States at their request or at the Committee's initiative.

The supervisory procedure is carried out in two stages: I. Finding of violation or non-violation (decision of the European Committee of Social Rights) II. Compliance with the Charter (follow-up to decisions).

STAGE I - DECISIONS OF THE EUROPEAN COMMITTEE OF SOCIAL RIGHTS

The European Committee of Social Rights (see its composition below) examines the reports submitted by the States and gives a legal ruling on the way in which those States have complied with their commitments. Its decisions are known as "conclusions".

The decisions of the European Committee of Social Rights are forwarded to the States. They are public and may be consulted on the Internet.[4]

Finding of compliance with the Charter. However, the Committee may put questions to the governments to which they must reply in their next report.

Finding of non-compliance with the Charter. The measures necessary to remedy the situation depend on the origin and the nature of the violation

---

[1] Affiliated to the European Trade Union Confederation (ETUC), the Union of Industrial and Employers' Confederations of Europe (UNICE) and the International Organisation of Employers (IOE).

[2] For practical reasons, the reports were forwarded to the organisations concerned until 1999 and then made freely available on the Charter's Internet site from 2000 onwards (www.esc.coe.int).

[3] Rule 18 of the Rules of procedure:

> 1. The Committee may decide to organise meetings with representatives of a State, as provided for in Article 24 paragraph 3 of the Charter as amended by the 1991 Amending Protocol, either on its own initiative or at the request of the State concerned. The Committee shall decide whether or not to act upon a request made by a State.
>
> 2. The international organisations of employers and trade unions referred to in Article 27 paragraph 2 of the Charter shall be invited to participate in these meetings. These organisations shall inform their national member organisations.
>
> 3. The meetings shall be public unless the President decides otherwise.

[4] www.esc.coe.int

(legislation, administrative practice, case law, etc.). The main progress made or underway following a decision of the European Committee of Social Rights or in the general context of commitments undertaken under the Charter is set out below in the survey by country.

Deferral of the decision. This occurs where the Committee does not have sufficient information to make a finding. The necessary data must be provided in the next report, failing which the Committee may adopt a finding of non-compliance on the ground that the State in question has not shown that it was complying with the Charter.

STAGE II – FOLLOW-UP TO DECISIONS AND COMPLIANCE

In the event that it is not envisaged to remedy a violation and take action on a decision of non-compliance, the Committee of Ministers may decide to address a recommendation to the State concerned (recommendations adopted are listed below D. Rcommendations adopted by the Committee of Ministers). A recommendation calls on the State concerned to take appropriate measures to remedy the situation.

The Committee of Ministers takes its decisions by a majority of two-thirds of those entitled to vote, namely the Contracting Parties to the Charter and the revised Charter. The recommendation is adopted if a majority of the Contracting parties to the Charter or the revised Charter has voted in favour.

The work of the Committee of Ministers is prepared by the Governmental Committee composed of representatives of the governments of the Contracting Parties to the Charter and assisted by representatives of the European social partners participating as observers.[1] When the Governmental Committee considers decisions of non-compliance – in the months following their publication – the State concerned must be in a position to set out the measures which it has taken or which it is contemplating taking in order to remedy the situation and, in the latter case, has to provide a timetable for achieving compliance.

DURATION OF THE PROCEDURE

The Committee of Ministers has fixed precise durations for the two stages of the procedure and hence for the performance of the functions of the European Committee of Social Rights and of the Governmental Committee (see below, C. Deadlines).

---

[1] Listed on page 30, footnote no. 1.

2. Collective complaints procedure[1]

This procedure enables collective complaints alleging violations of the Charter or of the revised Charter to be made to the European Committee of Social Rights.

Protocol No. 3, which provides for this procedure, entered into force on 1 July 1998.

The following organisations may submit complaints against any State having accepted the collective complaints procedure:

–   international non-governmental organisations with Council of Europe consultative status registered on a list drawn up for that purpose by the Governmental Committee;[2]
–   the European social partners.[3]

The following organisations may lodge complaints against the State within the jurisdiction of which they operate:

–   national employers' organisations and trade unions;
–   national non-governmental organisations (NGOs) if the State concerned has made a declaration authorising them to do so and they have particular competence in the relevant matters.[4]

The supervisory procedure is carried out in two stages: I. Finding of violation or non-violation (decisions of the European Committee of Social Rights) II. Compliance with the Charter (follow-up to decisions).

STAGE I. DECISION OF THE EUROPEAN COMMITTEE OF SOCIAL RIGHTS

Consideration of admissibility

The admissibility criteria relate to the organisations authorised to appeal (see above) and the formal conditions attaching to a claim.

Complaints have to be made in writing and signed by a person authorised to represent the complainant organisation.

---

[1] A chronological list of complaints is set out in this Chapter.

[2] The organisation concerned has to send a letter to the Secretariat of the European Social Charter – Directorate-General for Human Rights – DGII – Council of Europe – F-67705- Strasbourg Cedex (France). The letter must be accompanied by detailed documentation, including the statutes of the organisation, its sphere of activity, its objectives and its methods of operation. The resulting files are forwarded to the Governmental Committee for its decision. The list may be consulted on the Charter's Internet site www.esc.coe.int

[3] Listed on page 30 in footnote no. 1.

[4] Finland has made such a declaration.

Complaints made by the ETUC, UNICE, the IOE and INGOs must be made in one of the official languages of the Council of Europe (English or French). Complaints made by national employers' organisations and trade unions or by national non-governmental organisations of the Contracting Party concerned may be made in the official language of the defendant state.

Complaints must include the following information:

– the name and contact details of the complainant organisation;
– in the case of NGOs, reference to its Council of Europe consultative status and its registration on the list drawn up by the Governmental Committee, together with the areas of activity in which the organisation has competence;
– the State challenged, which must have accepted the collective complaints procedure;
– the Charter provisions relied upon: the State in respect of which the complaint is made must have accepted those provisions;
– the purpose of the complaint, indicating the extent to which the country concerned has failed to ensure the satisfactory application of the Charter and the relevant arguments. Copies of relevant documents are required.

There is no requirement for domestic remedies to have been exhausted. A complaint may be declared admissible even if the point of law at issue is being, or has already been, submitted to another national or international authority. Likewise, the fact that the point of law to which the complaint relates has already been examined under the report procedure does not *per se* preclude its admissibility.

The proceedings are *inter partes*. The State and the complainant organisation are requested by the Committee to submit written observations on admissibility. This is optional, since the Committee can decide of its own motion to reject a complaint which is manifestly inadmissible.

Consideration of the merits

The procedure for the consideration of the merits is also *inter partes*. It takes the form of exchanges of written comments or memorials from the complainant organisation and the defendant State, and also from other States which have accepted the collective complaints procedure and from the social partners. Each party is entitled to respond to the comments of the others.

The Committee may also organise hearings involving the parties to the complaint of its own initiative or at the parties' request. Hearings are public.

Once it has all the information, the Committee draws up a report for the Committee of Ministers of the Council of Europe which contains its decision on the merits and rules on whether the State has or has not complied with the Charter.

The report is forwarded to the Committee of Ministers and notified to the complainant organisation and the States which have ratified the Charter or the revised Charter, although they are not entitled to publish it. The report is made public no later than four months after it was forwarded to the Committee of Ministers (see below).

STAGE II. FOLLOW-UP TO DECISIONS AND COMPLIANCE

At the end of the procedure, the Committee of Ministers adopts a resolution. Where appropriate, it may make a recommendation to the State complained of to take specific measures to bring the situation into compliance with the Charter (the recommendations adopted are listed below, D. Recommendation adopted by the Committee of Ministers).

The resolution is adopted by a majority of votes cast and the recommendation by two-thirds of votes cast, only States which have ratified the Charter and the revised Charter being entitled to take part in the vote.

Once the Committee of Ministers has adopted its resolution or recommendation, the report is forwarded to the Parliamentary Assembly and made public.[1] The Protocol stipulates a time from which the report must be made public in any event: four months after it has been forwarded to the Committee of Ministers.

The State must report on measures taken to bring the situation into compliance with the Charter in its next report on the Charter.

DURATION OF THE PROCEDURE

The average duration of proceedings before the European Committee of Social Rights in complaints 1/1999 to 8/2000 was 18 months.

---

[1] Reports to the Committee of Ministers may be consulted on the Charter's Internet site www.esc.coe.int

LIST OF COMPLAINTS (AS OF 1ST AUGUST 2001)

No. 1/1998   **International Commission of jurists v. Portugal**
The complaint relates to Article 7§1 of the Charter (prohibition to work for children under 15 years). It alleges that the situation in practice in Portugal is in violation of this provision.

The European Committee of Social Rights transmitted its report containing its decision on the merits of the complaint to the Committee of Ministers on 10 September 1999. The Committee of Ministers adopted Resolution ChS (99)4 on 15 December 1999.

No. 2/1999   **European Federation of Employees in Public Services v. France**
The complaint relates to Articles 5 (the right to organise) and 6 (the right to bargain collectively) of the Charter. It alleges that the armed forces are denied these rights.

The European Committee of Social Rights transmitted the report containing its decision on the merits of the complaint to the Committee of Ministers on 12 December 2000. The Committee of Ministers adopted Resolution ChS(2001)2 on 7 February 2001.

No. 3/1999   **European Federation of Employees in Public Services v. Greece**
The complaint relates to Articles 5 (the right to organise) and 6 (the right to bargain collectively) of the Charter. It alleges that the armed forces are denied these rights.

The European Committee of Social Rights declared the complaint inadmissible on 13 October 1999.

No. 4/1999   **European Federation of Employees in Public Services v. Italy**
The complaint relates to Articles 5 (the right to organise) and 6 (the right to bargain collectively) of the Charter. It alleges that the armed forces are denied these rights.

The European Committee of Social Rights transmitted the report containing its decision on the merits of the complaint to the Committee of Ministers on 12 December 2000. The Committee of Ministers adopted Resolution ChS(2001)3 on 7 February 2001.

No. 5/1999   **European Federation of Employees in Public Services v. Portugal**
The complaint relates to Articles 5 (the right to organise) and 6 (the right to bargain collectively) of the Charter. It alleges that the armed forces are denied these rights.

The European Committee of Social Rights transmitted the report containing its decision on the merits of the complaint to the Committee of Ministers on 12 December 2000. The Committee of Ministers adopted Resolution ChS(2001)4 on 7 February 2001.

No. 6/1999   **Syndicat national des professions du tourisme v. France**
The complaint relates to Articles 1 (para. 2) (prohibition against all forms of discrimination in access to employment), 10 (the right to vocational training) and E (non-discrimination) of the revised Charter. It alleges discrimination in access to work and vocational training for guide-interpreters and national lecturers.

The European Committee of Social Rights transmitted the report containing its decision on the merits of the complaint to the Committee of Ministers on 13 October 2000. The Committee of Ministers adopted Recommendation n° R ChS(2001)1 on 30 January 2001.

No. 7/2000   **International Federation of Human Rights Leagues v. Greece**
The complaint relates to Article 1 (para. 2) (prohibition of forced labour) of the Charter. It alleges that a number of legislative provisions and regulations do not respect the prohibition of forced labour.

The European Committee of Social Rights transmitted the report containing its decision on the merits of the complaint to the Committee of Ministers on 12 December 2000. The Committee of Ministers adopted Resolution ChS(2001)6 on 5 April 2001.

No. 8/2000   **Quaker Council for European Affairs v. Greece**
The complaint relates to Article 1 (para. 2) (prohibition of forced labour) of the Charter. It alleges that the application in practice of the act authorising alternative forms of military service for conscientious objectors does not respect the prohibition of forced labour.

The European Committee of Social Rights transmitted the report containing its decision on the merits of the complaint to the Committee of Ministers on 27 April 2001.

No. 9/2000   **Confédération Française de l'Encadrement – CGC v. France**
The complaint relates to Articles 2 (the right to just conditions of work), 4 (the right to a fair remuneration), 6 (the right to bargain collectively including the right to strike) and 27 (the right of workers with family responsibilities to equal opportunities and equal treatment) of the revised Charter. It alleges that the provisions relating to the working hours of white-collar workers contained in the second Act on the Reduction of Working Hours (Act No. 2000-37 of 19 January 2000 –

"Loi Aubry n° 2") violates these provisions.

The European Committee of Social Rights declared the complaint admissible on 6 November 2000

No. 10/2000   **Tehy ry and STTK ry v. Finland**
The complaint relates to Article 2 para. 4 (the right to additional paid holidays or reduced working hours for workers engaged in dangerous or unhealthy occupations) of the European Social Charter. It alleges that the fact that hospital personnel who are subjected to the hazards of radiation during the course of their work are no longer entitled to special leave due to the exposure to radiation, violates this provision of the Charter.

The European Committee of Social Rights transmitted the report containing its decision on the merits of the complaint to the Committee of Ministers on 17 October 2001.

No. 11/2001   **European Council of Police Trade Unions v. Portugal**
The complaint relates to Articles 5 (right to organise) and 6 (right to collective bargaining). It alleges that members of Polícia de Segurança Pública are not guaranteed these rights.

The European Committee of Social Rights declared the complaint admissible on 17 October 2001.

C. Deadlines (reporting procedure)
1. European Social Charter (1961)

Reference Period	Date of submission of reports	Provisions	Conclusions of European Committee of Social Rights	Report of Governmental Committee	Decisions of the Committee of Ministers
XVI-1 1999-2000	30 June 2001	Hard core	28 February 2002	October 2002	December 2002
XVI-2 1997-2000	30 June 2001, or 31 March 2002	2nd half of remaining Articles	31 December 2002	October 2003	December 2003
XVII-1 2001-2002	30 June 2003	Hard core	28 February 2004	October 2004	December 2004
XVII-2 1999-2002	30 June 2003, or 31 March 2004	1st half of remaining Articles	31 December 2004	October 2005	December 2005

2. Revised Charter (1996)

Publication of Conclusions	Date of submission of reports	Provisions	Reference period[1]	France, Italy, Romania Slovenia and Sweden	Bulgaria	Cyprus, Estonia, Ireland, Lithuania, Norway	States ratifying between 1/7/2001 and 31/3/2002
2002	30 June 2001	Hard core	1999-2000	1st report			
2003	31 March 2002	First part of other provisions	1999-2000	**2nd report[2]**	**1st report[2]**		
2004	30 June 2003	Hard core	2001-2002	3rd report	2nd report	1st report	
2005	31 March 2004	Second part of other provisions	2001-2002	4th report	3rd report	**2nd report[2]**	**1st report[2]**
2006	30 June 2005	Hard core	2003-2004	5th report	4th report	3rd report	2nd report
2007	31 March 2006	First part of other provisions	2001-2004	6th report	5th report	4th report	3rd report
2008	30 June 2007	Hard core	2005-2006	7th report	6th report	5th report	4th report
2009	31 March 2008	Second part of other provisions	2003-2006	8th report	7th report	6th report	5th report

[1] To be adapted according to the date of entry in force of the revised Social Charter for each state.
[2] The reports in bold indicate that the first report exceptionally covers all the non-hard core provisions.

D. RECOMMENDATIONS ADOPTED BY THE COMMITTEE OF MINISTERS

1. Procedure of reports

Article 29 of the Charter provides that the Committee of Ministers of the Council of Europe may make any necessary recommendations to the States (see above). The first time this procedure was used was in 1993. To date, the Committee of Ministers has adopted 33 recommendations, which have been addressed to 14 States, 12 of these recommendations have been renewed at least once. The substance of each recommendation is indicated below. The full texts are to be found on the website: http://www.esc.coe.int.

Recommendations adopted on 7 September 1993
Supervision cycle XII-1

Greece RecChS(93)1 (renewed on 15 January 1997 and 4 March 1999 as far as Article 1§2 is concerned)
Article 1§2:   forced labour – merchant navy, armed forces
Article 13§1:   no individual right to social assistance
Article 13§4:   discrimination against non-nationals

Norway RecChS(93)2 (renewed on 14 December 1995 as far as Article 7§3 is concerned)
Article 6§4:   unjustified arbitration used in nurses' strike
Article 7§3:   possibility of an unduly long working week for
                              schoolchildren

United Kingdom RecChS(93)3
Article 6§4:   possibility of dismissal of strikers and selective re-hiring
Article 8§1:   inadequate maternity benefits

Recommendations adopted on 8 April 1994
Supervision cycle XII-2

Austria RecChs(94)1
Article 5:   no protection against dismissal on grounds of trade union
                              activities in firms with less than 5 employees
Article 8§2:   possibility of dismissing domestic employees after fifth
                              month of pregnancy

France RecChS(94)2 (renewed on 15 January 1997)
Article 1§2:   forced labour – merchant navy

Germany RecChS(94)3 (renewed on 4 March 1999 and 5 September 2001)
Article 19§6:   various restrictions on family reunion

Italy RecChS(94)4 (renewed on 14 December 1995 as far as Articles 7§1 and 13§1 concerned and on 15 January as far as Articles 1§, 3§2 and 4§5 are concerned))
Article 1§2:   forced labour - merchant navy, civil aviation
Article 3§2:   failure to provide necessary information for an assessment of the situation
Article 4§4:   inadequate periods of notice of dismissal in certain sectors
Article 4§5:   no regulation of wage deductions
Article 7§1:   no prohibition on work of young persons under fifteen in agriculture and domestic work
Article 8§1:   no paid maternity leave for domestic workers
Article 8§2:   possibility of dismissal of domestic workers during maternity leave
Article 8§3:   no entitlement to paid nursing breaks for domestic employees and home workers
Article 13§1:   no individual right to social assistance

Spain RecChS(94)5
Article 1§2:   forced labour - merchant navy, civil aviation

Recommendations adopted on 22 May 1995
Supervision cycle XIII-1

Austria RecChS(95)1
Article 5:   no protection against dismissal on grounds of trade union activities in firms with less than five employees
Article 8§2:   possibility of dismissing domestic employees after fifth month of pregnancy

Denmark RecChS(95)2
Article 5:   restrictions on right of association under Danish International Ships' Register
Article 6§2:   restrictions on collective bargaining, and unequal treatment under Danish International Ships' Register
Article 6§4:   no right to strike for civil servants

France RecChS(95)3 (renewed on 15 January 1997)
Article 1§2:   forced labour - merchant navy

Greece RecChS(95)4 (renewed on 15 January 1997 and 4 March 1999 as far as Article 1§2 is concerned) / RecChS(95)5

Article 1§2:	forced labour - merchant navy, armed forces
Article 7§1:	no minimum age for employment in agricultural, forestry or livestock work in family undertakings
Article 7§3:	no minimum age for employment in agricultural, forestry or livestock work in family undertakings
Article 19§1:	failure to provide necessary information for an assessment of the situation
Article 19§8:	no right of appeal against a deportation order

Ireland RecChS(95)6 (renewed on 14 December 1995, 4 March 1999 and 7 February 2001 as far as Article 19§8 is concerned)

Article 1§2:	forced labour, merchant navy
Article 4§4:	inadequate periods of notice of termination of employment
Article 6§4:	insufficient protection for merchant seamen on strike
Article 7§3:	insufficient regulation of working hours for children in the employment of a relative
Article 19§8:	no right of appeal against a deportation order

Italy RecChS(95)7(renewed on 15 January 1997 as far as Articles 1§2, 3§2 and 4§5 are concerned)/ RecChS(95)8

Article 1§2:	forced labour - merchant navy, civil aviation
Article 3§1:	certain self-employed workers without protection in matters of health and safety
Article 3§2:	certain self-employed workers without protection in matters of health and safety
Article 3§2:	failure to provide necessary information for an assessment of the situation
Article 4§4:	inadequate periods of notice of dismissal in certain sectors
Article 4§5:	no regulation of wage deductions

Spain RecChS(95)9

Article 1§2:	forced labour - merchant navy and aviation crew

Sweden RecChS(95)10 (renewed on 14 December 1995)

Article 19§8:	no right of appeal against deportation order

Recommendations adopted on 14 December 1995
Supervision cycle XIII-2

Greece RecChS(95)11

Article 18§2:	failure to simplify procedures in respect of non-EU/EEA migrants

Italy RecChS(95)12

Article 7§4:	inadequate regulation of working hours for persons under 16 years of age

Recommendations adopted on 15 January 1997
Supervision Cycle XIII-3

Malta RecChS(97)1

Articles 5 and
6§2:   obligation on police to join Maltese Police Association. Impossibility of their affiliating with another union or association

Turkey RecChS(97)2

Article 7§3:	certain sectors not subject to prohibition on child labour

United Kingdom RecChS(97)3

Article 1§2:	forced labour - merchant navy

Articles 5 and
6§2:   legislative restrictions on freedom of association and collective bargaining

Articles 6§4:	possibility of dismissal of strikers and selective re-hiring

Recommendations adopted on 4 February 1998
Supervision cycle XIII-4

France RecChS(98)1

Article 17:	Inequality of inheritance rights for children born in adultery

Germany RecChS(98)2

Article 6§4:	restriction on the right to strike

Italy RecChS(98)3

Article 7§2:	minimum age too low for certain dangerous occupations (benzene)

Turkey RecChS(98)4 (renewed on 7 February 2001 as far as Article 16 is concerned)
Article 11:   excessive infant and childbirth death rate
Article 16:   inequalities between parents and low proportion of families benefiting from family allowances

Recommendations adopted on 2 July 1998
Supervision cycle XIII-5

Portugal RecChS(98)5
Article 7§1:   No practical compliance with the prohibition of work for children under fifteen.

Recommendations adopted on 4 March 1999
Supervision cycle XIV-1

Austria RecChS(99)1 (renewed on 7 February 2001)
Article 5:   election to works councils restricted to nationals

Ireland RecChS(99)2 (renewed on 7 February 2001)
Article 5
and 6§2:   legislative restrictions on freedom of association and collective bargaining

Recommendations adopted on 27 October 1999
Supervision cycle XIV-2

Turkey RecChS(99)3
Article 4§3:   no prohibition of wage discrimination between women and men in certain sectors of the economy

Recommendations adopted on 7 February 2001
Supervision cycle XV-1

Ireland RecChS(2001)2
Article 6§4 :   lack of protection for workers on strike

Malta RecChS(2001)3
Article 5 and
Article 6§2:   restrictions on trade union membership within the Police

2. Collective complaints procedure

Portugal

Article 7§1: Complaint No. 1/1998
International Commission of Jurists v. Portugal
Resolution ChS (99)4 adopted on 15 December 1999
referring to RecChS (98)5 (see above)

France

Article 1§2: Complaint No. 6/1999
Syndicat national des Professions du Tourisme v. France
RecChS (2001)1 : employment discrimination

Greece

Article 1§2: Complaint No. 7/2000
International Federation of Human Rights Leagues v. Greece
Resolution ChS(2001)6 adopted on 5 April 2001
referring to RecChS (93)1 and (95)4 (see above)

III. Survey by country

— Austria —

Austria ratified the European Social Charter on 29/10/1969. Austria has accepted 62 of the Charter's 72 paragraphs.

Austria ratified the Protocol No. 2 reforming the control mechanism on 13/071995.

Austria has signed but not yet ratified the Protocol No.1 which adds new rights, the Protocol No. 3 on "collective complaints" and the revised Charter.

Between 1992 and 2000, Austria has submitted 18 reports on the application of the Charter. The 19th report on the hard core provisions was submitted on 11/07/2001.

Austria's record with respect to application of the Charter is the following as of 1 July 2001:

Examples of progress achieved or being achieved

Employment
▶ Repealing of the 1885 Vagrancy Act and of Article 305 of the Criminal Code (Act of 1 January 1975) *Article 1§2 – prohibition of forced labour*

Social Protection
▶ The punishment for the abuse of children under 14 years of age was increased, and in the case of certain sexual offences committed against children, the statute of limitations does not begin to run until the age of majority has been reached (amendments made in 1998 to the criminal law on sexual offences) *Articles 7§10 and 17 – rights of young persons (legal and social protection).*

Movement of persons
▶ Under the terms of the Association Agreement between Turkey and the EU and the decision taken by the Association Council in 1998, children of Turkish residents legally employed in the labour market are now entitled to the exemption certificate allowing them to work anywhere in Austria once they have lived in the country for five years. *Article 18§2 – right to simplification and liberalisation of formalities related to immigration.*

Equality

▶ The prohibition of discrimination against the disabled was introduced into the Austrian Federal Constitution on 9 July 1997. *Article 1§2 – prohibition discrimination in employment.*

▶ A worker is allowed to take legal action before a court to ensure the observance of the equal pay for women and men principle (Act of 23 February 1979 on equality of treatment). *Article 4§3 – right to equal pay.*

Cases of non-compliance

Equality (nationality)

Discrimination against non EU or EEA[1] nationals in the following matters:

▶ No access to apprenticeships. *Articles 1§4 and 10§2 – right of access to apprenticeship.*

▶ No eligibility for election to works councils. *Article 5 - right to organise.*

▶ No benefit of subsidies for housing construction. *Article 16 - rights of the family (housing).*

▶ Granting of family allowances subject to the condition of being gainfully employed for at least three months and to a residence requirement for children (Family Burdens Equalisation Act of 24 October 1997). *Articles 12§4 and 16 – right of equal treatment in respect with family benefits.*

▶ More restrictive conditions of entitlement to emergency assistance. *Article 12§4 – right to equal treatment in social security matters.*

Movement of persons

▶ *Article 19§6 – right to family reunion* 1. Nationals of countries not member states of the EU or parties to the EEA who settled in Austria before 1 January 1998 (date of the entry into force of the new Aliens Act) may only benefit from family reunion for children under 14 years of age; 2. Since 1 January 1998, migrants who do not request family reunion within one calendar year of obtaining a residence permit can also only benefit from family reunion for children aged under 14.

---

[1] The European Union (EU) and the European Economic Area (EEA).

— Belgium —

Belgium ratified the European Social Charter on 16/10/1990. Belgium has accepted all of the Charter's 72 paragraphs.

Belgium ratified Protocol No. 2 reforming the control mechanism on 21/09/2000. Belgium has signed but not yet ratified Protocol No. 1 which adds new rights, the revised Charter and Protocol No. 3 on "collective complaints".

Between 1992 and 2000, Belgium submitted 5 reports on the application of the Charter. The next report on the hard core provisions was due on 30/06/2001.

Belgium's record with respect to application of the Charter is the following as of 1 July 2001:

Examples of progress achieved or being achieved

Social Protection
▶ Amendment of the rules governing remands in custody for young people (repeal of Article 53 of the Act on the Protection of Young Persons of 8 April 1965 by the Act of 4 May 1999). *Articles 7§10 and 17 – rights of young persons(legal and social protection).*

Movement of Persons
▶ Bill for the abolition of charges for applications for authorisation to work and work permits. *Article 18§2 – right to simplification and liberalisation of formalities related to immigration.*

Employment
▶ Bill amending the Disciplinary and Criminal Code for the Merchant Navy and Maritime Fishing . *Article 1§2 – prohibition of forced labour .*
▶ The Act of 4 December 1998 places a limit on weekly working hours in the "extensive flexibility scheme." *Article 2§1 – right to reasonable working time*
▶ The collective agreement of 20 December 1999 extended periods of notice for workers. *Article 4§4 – right to notice on dismissal.*

Cases of non-compliance
Health
▶ *Article 2§4 – right to compensatory time off in dangerous occupations.* There is no system for reducing working time or giving additional paid leave for those employed in dangerous or unhealthy occupations.

▶ *Article 11§3 – right to health protection: regulations and prophylactic measures.* Rates of vaccination against a number of diseases are inadequate to ensure effective protection against those diseases in accordance with WHO objectives.

Equality (nationality)

Discrimination against non EU or EEA nationals in the following matters:

▶ Grant of family benefits under the general scheme for employees (subject to children's residence), guaranteed family benefits and disability benefits (conditions relating to length of residence) and export of old-age pensions acquired in Belgium.

Articles 12§4 and 16 – right of equal treatment in respect of family benefits.

▶ Financial assistance granted in higher education.

Article 10§4 – right to vocational training.

▶ Access to a number of services and benefits for disabled persons.

Article 15§1/2 – right of disabled persons to employment and training.

Movement of persons

▶ *Article 19§6 – right to family reunion.* Partial reunion of families is prohibited. The Government has not shown that children aged between 18 and 21 are eligible in practice for family reunion.

Employment

▶ *Article 1§2 – prohibition of forced labour.* Criminal sanctions are laid down for disciplinary offences committed by seamen even where the safety of a vessel or the lives or health of persons on board is not in danger.

▶ *Article 2§1 – right to reasonable working time.* The provisions regulating the "limited flexibility" scheme do not provide sufficient guarantees of collective bargaining to protect workers.

▶ *Article 4§2 – right to increased remuneration for overtime work.* Insufficient compensation for overtime work in the public sector

▶ *Article 7§5 –right of young employees to special working conditions (remuneration).* The amount withheld from apprentices' wages in their first year of apprenticeship is excessive in relation to the statutory minimum wage for adults.

▶ *Article 8§2 – prohibition of dismissal during maternity leave.* Reinstatement is not the rule in the event of unlawful dismissal of the employee in question and the compensation payable is not sufficiently dissuasive for employers.

▶ *Article 8§3 – right to time off for nursing mothers.* There is no legal obligation to give employees time off for nursing during working hours.

— Bulgaria —

Bulgaria ratified the revised European Social Charter on 07/06/2000 and has accepted 61 of the revised Charter's 98 paragraphs.

Bulgaria has agreed to be bound by the "collective complaints" procedure. It has not yet made a declaration enabling national NGOs to submit complaints.

The first report, on half of the provisions outside of the hard core of the revised Charter, is due on 31/03/2002.

— Cyprus —

Cyprus ratified the European Social Charter on 07/03/1968 and the revised Charter on 27/09/2000. Cyprus accepted 34 of the 72 paragraphs of the Charter at the time of its ratification in 1968 and has gradually extended this to 43 paragraphs, including 23 of the 28 hard core paragraphs. It has accepted 66 of the 98 paragraphs of the revised Charter, having first denounced two of the provisions of the 1961 Charter.

Cyprus ratified Protocol No. 2 reforming the control mechanism on 01/06/1993 and Protocol No. 3 on "collective complaints" on 06/08/1996. It has not yet made a declaration enabling national NGOs to submit collective complaints.

Between 1970 and 2000, Cyprus submitted 19 reports on the application of the Social Charter. The 20th report pertaining to the hard core provisions of the Social Charter was submitted on 27/08/2001.

Cyprus's record with respect to application of the Charter is the following as of 1 July 2001:

Examples of progress achieved or being achieved

Health

▶ Regulation of the right to maternity leave (Act No. 54/1987 on maternity protection, as amended by Act No. 48 (I) /1994); extension of maternity leave to sixteen weeks (Act No. 100 (I) 97 on maternity protection). *Article 8§1 – right to maternity leave.*

▶ Regulation of health and safety in agriculture and extension of the Labour Inspectorate's purview to include this sector (Act No. 22/1982). *Article 3§1 and 2 – right to health and safety at work – regulations and supervision.*

▶ Water and air pollution monitoring (1991 Acts). *Article 11§1 – right of access to health.*

Health/Education

▶ Prohibition of the employment of children under the age of 15 (1990 Act amending the Employment of Children and Young Persons Act) and compulsory schooling for all children up to the age of 15 or until they have completed lower secondary education (Primary and Secondary Education Act No. 24/1993). *Article 7§1 and 3 – prohibition of the employment of children under 15.*

▶ Extension of the prohibition of night work for young persons under the age of majority to include all activities (act amending the Employment of Children and Young Persons Act, date of entry into force: 9 July 1999). *Article 7§8 – rights of children – night work.*

Employment/Right to Organise

▶ Abolition of criminal sanctions and other coercive measures as "disciplinary occupational measures" for seafarers (Act of 11 June 1976 amending the Merchant Shipping Act). *Article 1§2 – prohibition of forced labour.*

▶ Regulation of the prohibition of dismissal during maternity leave (Maternity Protection Act No. 54/1987, as amended by Act No. 48 (I) of 1994); possibility of court-ordered reinstatement for unlawfully dismissed employees in firms with twenty or more employees (Act No. 61 (I) 1994). *Article 8§2 – prohibition of dismissal during maternity leave.*

▶ Abolition of restrictions on trade unions' right to elect their own representatives freely (Act No. 381/1991 amending the Trade Unions Act); protection of union membership (Termination of Employment Acts 1967-1994 and the Trade Unions Acts 1965-1996). *Article 5 – the right to organise.*

▶ Safeguarding of police officers' right to bargain collectively (Section 52 §1 of the 1989 Police Act No. 27). *Article 5 – right to organise and Article 6 – right to bargain collectively.*

Social Protection

▶ Introduction of a proper system of social security (Act No. 106/1972); draft law presented to Parliament on 25 February 1999 with a view to introducing universal coverage in the field of healthcare. *Article 12§1 – right to social security (establishment and maintenance of a social security system).*

Movement of Persons

▶ Guarantees in the event of expulsion (Aliens and Immigration Act No. 54/1976). *Article 19§8 – right to guarantees in the event of expulsion.*

Equality

Sex

▶ Equal pay for work of equal value (Act No. 158/1989, entered into force in 1992). *Article 4§3 – right to equal pay.*

Nationality

▶ Additional supervisory measures to secure genuine equality in the treatment of foreigners with respect to employment (government provisions 1989-1990). *Article 19§4 – right to equality of treatment in respect of employment.*

Cases of non-compliance

Employment

▶ *Article 1§2 – prohibition of forced labour.* Defence Regulation 79A grants the Cabinet or any given minister the power to requisition workers in a number of instances, while Defence Regulation 79B allows the Cabinet to pass decrees banning strikes. These regulations allow curbs and restrictions over and above those permitted under Article 31 of the Charter.

▶ *Article 8§2 – prohibition of dismissal during maternity leave.* The possibility of court-ordered reinstatement for female employees who have been unlawfully dismissed has not been extended to women working in firms with fewer than twenty employees.

Equality (nationality)

▶ *Article 12§4 – right to social security.* 1. The social pension (Act No. 25 (I) 95) is subject to an unreasonable length-of-residence requirement. 2. The principle of aggregation of insurance or employment periods is not applied to all nationals of Contracting Parties to the Charter.

— The Czech Republic —

The Czech Republic ratified the European Social Charter on 03/11/1999 and Protocol No. 1 which adds new rights on 17/11/1999. The Czech Republic has accepted 52 of the Charter's 72 paragraphs and the 4 paragraphs of Protocol No. 1.

The Czech Republic has signed but not yet ratified the revised Charter.

The Czech Republic ratified Protocol No. 2 reforming the control mechanism on 17/11/1999. It has not signed or ratified Protocol No. 3 on "collective complaints"

The first report, on the hard core provisions of the Charter, was submitted on 22/10/2001.

— Denmark —

Denmark ratified the European Social Charter on 03/03/1965 and Protocol No. 1 which adds new rights on 27/08/1996. Denmark has accepted 45 of the 72 paragraphs of the Charter as well as the 4 paragraphs of the Protocol.

Denmark has signed but not yet ratified the revised Charter and Protocol No. 3 on "collective complaints".

Between 1968 and 2000, Denmark has submitted 20 reports on the application of the Charter. The next report on the hard core provisions was due on 30/06/2001.

Denmark's record with respect to application of the Charter is the following as of 1 July 2001:

Examples of progress achieved or being achieved

Employment
▶ Sections 198 and 199 of the Criminal Code which provided for criminal sanctions to be applied in cases of deliberate idleness or lack of means of subsistence were repealed (Act No. 141/1999). *Article 1§2 - prohibition of forced labour.*
▶ Strengthened protection against dismissal on grounds related to association membership (Act No. 285/1982 amended by Act No. 443/1990). *Article 5 – right to organise.*

Equality
▶ Prohibition of both direct and indirect discrimination in the labour market with regard to race, colour, religion, political opinion, sexual orientation and national, social or ethnic origin (1996 Act on prohibition against discrimination in the labour market). *Article 1§2 – prohibition of discrimination in employment.*

Cases of non-compliance

Health
▶*Article 8§1 – right to maternity benefits and leave.* Legislation does not provide for a compulsory post-natal leave period of at least 6 weeks.

Employment
▶*Article 5 - right to organise.* 1. Legislation permits the dismissal of a worker who refuses to join a trade union if, at the time of his engagement, he knew that his employment was conditional on membership of the trade union. 2. It also permits the dismissal of a worker who refuses to continue as a member of a particular trade union after being informed subsequent to his engagement that membership was a condition for continued employment.

▶*Articles 5 and 6§2 – right to collective action (machinery for voluntary negotiation).* Legislation on the Danish International Ship's Register provides that collective agreements on wages and working conditions concluded by Danish trade unions are only applicable to seafarers resident in Denmark.

▶*Article 6§4 - right to collective bargaining (strikes and lock-outs).* Civil servants do not have the right to strike.

Movement of persons
▶*Article 18§3 – right to simplification and liberalisation of formalities related to immigration.* Rules which provide for the revoking of a work permit granted to a foreigner for a particular post with a particular employer if he/she changes employer are too restrictive

Equality (nationality)
Discrimination against non EU or EEA nationals in the following matters:
▶ Granting of family allowances (subject to a residence requirement of children)
Articles 12§4 and 16 – right to equal treatment with respect to family benefits.
▶ No accumulation of periods of insurance or employment.
Article 12§4 – right to equal treatment in social security matters.
▶No entitlement to long term social and medical assistance.
Article 13§1 – individual right to adequate assistance.

— Estonia —

Estonia ratified the revised European Social Charter on 11/09/2000 and has accepted 79 of the revised Charter's 98 paragraphs.

Estonia has not agreed to be bound by the "collective complaints" procedure.

The first report, on the hard core provisions of the revised Charter, is due on 30/06/2003.

— Finland —

Finland ratified the European Social Charter and Protocol No. 1 which adds new rights on 29/04/1991. Finland has accepted 62 of the Charter's 72 paragraphs and the 4 paragraphs of Protocol No. 1.

Finland ratified Protocol No. 2 reforming the control mechanism on 18/08/1994 and Protocol No. 3 on "collective complaints" on 17/07/1998. Finland has made a declaration enabling national NGO's to submit complaints.

Finland has signed but not yet ratified the revised Charter.

Between 1993 and 2000, Finland submitted 6 reports on the application of the Charter. Finland submitted its 7th report, on the hard core provisions, on 16/08/2001.

Finland's record with respect to application of the Charter is the following as of 1 July 2001:

Examples of progress achieved or being achieved

Equality (nationality)

▶ Signature in Spring 2000 of a new collective agreement in the hotel and catering sectors, under which it is no longer necessary for shop stewards to be Finnish citizens. *Articles 5 and 19(4) – right to equal treatment in trade union matters.*

Employment

▶ Extension to private employment agencies of the principles applicable to public employment services (Act No. 1005/1993 as amended in 1999). *Article 1 §3 – right to free employment services.*

▶ The time for which children of 14 years and over who are subject to compulsory education may work has been set at half the school holidays. Employment of children of over 15 years of age for emergency work is possible only if no adult is available to carry it out. If the rest period of a young worker has been reduced on account of emergency work, a comparable rest period must be given to him as soon as possible within a period of no more than three weeks (Act No. 998/1993 as amended in 1999). *Article 7- right of young people between 15 and 18 years of age to special conditions of employment.*

Movement of persons

▶ *Article 18§4 – right to simplification and liberalisation of formalities related to immigration.* Repeal in 1998 of the provision of the 1986 Passports Act which made it possible to refuse a passport to "persons who prove unable to look after themselves"

Cases of non-compliance

Equality (nationality)

Discrimination against non EU and EEA nationals in the following matters:

▶   Granting of family allowances (subject to a children's residence requirement).

Articles 12§4 and 16 – right to equal treatment with respect to family benefits.

▶ Financial assistance granted for vocational training and higher education (condition relating to the duration of residence).

Article 10§4 – right to vocational training.

▶ No aggregation of periods of insurance or employment (not insured).

Article 12§4 – right to equal treatment in social security matters.

▶ Legal aid for bringing proceedings (requirement of permanent residence).

Article 19§7 –right to equal treatment in respect of legal proceedings

Employment

▶ *Article 2§1 - right to reasonable working time.* The legislation on working time enables daily rest periods during employment to be reduced to 7 or even 5 hours

▶ *Article 8§2 – prohibition of dismissal during maternity leave.* In practice, women unlawfully dismissed are rarely reinstated in their jobs by judicial decision and the damages granted are not sufficiently dissuasive for the employer or compensatory for the employee.

— France —

France ratified the European Social Charter on 09/03/1973 and the revised Charter on 07/05/1999. France has accepted all 98 paragraphs of the revised Charter.

France ratified Protocol No. 3 on "collective complaints" on 07/05/1999. It has not yet made a declaration enabling national NGOs to submit complaints.

Between 1975 and 2000, France submitted 16 reports on the application of the Charter. France submitted its first report on the hard core provisions of the revised Charter on 27/07/2001.

France's record with respect to application of the Charter is the following as of 1 July 2001:

Examples of progress achieved or being achieved

Health/Education

▶ Determination of a minimum age for employment in family businesses in the agricultural sector (Decree n° 97-370 of 14 April 1997) and in other sectors (Ordinance No. 2001-174 of 22 February 2001). *Article 7§1 – prohibition of employment of young people under 15 years of age.*

Equality

Nationality

▶ Abolition of the requirement for reciprocity to which the grant of AAH and of the FSV supplementary benefit was subject as far as foreign nationals were concerned (Act No. 98-349 of 11 May 1998). *Article 12§4 – right to social security.*

▶ Unqualified extension of reciprocity with regard to social assistance to cover all nationals of Contracting Parties to the Charter (Circulars of 21 August 1974 and 10 October 1989). *Article 13 – right to social assistance.*

▶ Access of foreign nationals without discrimination to positions in trade union administration and management (Act No. 82-915 of 28 October 1982). *Articles 5 and 19§4 – right to equal treatment in trade union matters.*

▶ Abolition of the security required to be lodged by foreign nationals bringing legal proceedings (Act No. 75-596 of 9 July 1975). *Article 19§7 – right to equal treatment in respect of bringing legal proceedings.*

Property
▶ Repeal of the Articles of the Electoral Code which prevent recipients of social assistance from being elected as municipal councillors (Act n° 75-534 of 30 June 1975). *Article 13§2 – right of recipients of assistance to non-discrimination in the exercise of social and political rights.*

Birth
▶ Revision of the Civil Code in February 2001 to eliminate all discrimination against children born out of wedlock where inheritance is concerned. *Article 17 – rights of young people (legal and social protection).*

Employment
▶ Repeal of provisions of the Criminal and Disciplinary Code governing the Merchant Navy which provided for penal sanctions for breach of discipline by seamen even when the safety of the vessel or the life or health of persons on board was not endangered (Draft Law on Social Modernisation 2001). *Article 1§2 - prohibition of forced labour.*

Movement of persons
▶ The classes of foreign nationals not subject to expulsion have been extended (Act of 2 August 1989). *Article 19§8 – entitlement to safeguards in the event of deportation.*

Cases of non-compliance

Equality
Discrimination against non EU or EEA nationals in the following matters:
▶ Granting of family allowances (subject to a children's residence requirement). *Articles 12§4 and 16 – right to equal treatment with respect to family benefits.*
▶ Grant of minimum integration income and certain other forms of social assistance provided by the Code on Families and Social Assistance (condition relating to duration of residence).
Article 13§1 – individual right to adequate social and medical assistance.

Education/Health
▶ *Article 7§3 – prohibition of the employment of children under 15 years of age.* Minors taking part in public performances during school holidays are not entitled to a minimum rest period.

Social Protection
▶ *Article 8§1 – right to maternity benefits.* Periods of unemployment are not taken into account as periods of employment for the purposes of entitlement to maternity benefits.

▶ *Article 13§1 – individual right to adequate social and medical assistance.* Young people under 25 years of age do not qualify for the minimum integration income (RMI) and the other measures of social assistance provided for them are not sufficient.

Employment/Right to organise

▶ *Article 1§2 – prohibition of discrimination in employment. Complaint 6/1999-Syndicat National des Professions du Tourisme v. France (Decision of 13 October 2000).* Multilingual guides and State registered national lecturers/guides are in practice subject to unjustified discrimination with regard to their ability to carry out visits and the rates applied to visit certain locations.

▶ *Article 4§4 - right to notice of dismissal.* The maximum two-month period of notice laid down by law is insufficient in the case of employees who have worked for a long period for the same employer.

▶ *Article 8§2 – prohibition of dismissal during maternity leave.* Employees are not generally reinstated in their former employment in the event of unlawful dismissal.

▶ *Article 8§3 – right to time off for nursing mothers.* Time off for nursing is not regarded as actual work and the employer is not under a duty to provide remuneration for such time.

▶ *Article 6§4 – right to bargain collectively (strikes and lockouts).* 1. The deductions for striking civil servants are not always proportional to the duration of the strike. 2. Only the most representative trade unions have the right to initiate collective action in the public sector.

— Germany —

Germany ratified the European Social Charter on 27/01/1965. Germany has accepted 67 of the Charter's 72 paragraphs.

Germany has signed but not yet ratified Protocol No. 1 which adds new rights.

Germany has neither signed nor ratified Protocol No. 2 reforming the control mechanism, Protocol No. 3 on "collective complaints" and the revised Charter.

Between 1968 and 2000, Germany has submitted 18 reports on the application of the Charter. The 19th report, on the hard core provisions of the Charter, was submitted on 06/11/2001.

Germany's record with respect to application of the Charter is the following as of 1 July 2001:

Examples of progress achieved or being achieved

Health

▶ Any employed woman giving birth prematurely, and thereby losing part of the compulsory six-week period of prenatal leave, benefits from an equivalent extension of her postnatal leave, thus receiving an effective total of twelve weeks' leave (Act of 20 December 1996 amending the Maternity Protection Act). *Article 8§1 – right to maternity benefits and leave.*

Employment

▶ Repealing of the provision allowing a crew member to be imprisoned if he wilfully refused to return to his post on board (Merchant Shipping Act of 29 October 1974). *Article 1§2 – prohibition of forced labour.*

Social Protection

▶ The Act on Equal Status under Succession Law (April 1998) and the Act to Reform Parent and Child Law (July 1998) abolished remaining differences in treatment of children born inside and outside wedlock. Measures were taken in 1998 to strengthen the protection of children from ill-treatment (for example the amendments to the law on child abuse and further increases in the penalties for child abuse, and for the dissemination of child pornography). *Articles 7§10 and 17 – rights of young persons to social and family development.*

Equality (sex)

▶ Amendments to the Civil Code by an Act of 19 December 1998 and to the Labour Court Act by an Act of 31 August 1998 in respect of rules on liability of employers in cases of gender discrimination. *Article 1§2 – prohibition of discrimination in employment.*

Cases of non-compliance

Employment

▶ *Article 6§4 - right to collective bargaining (strikes and lock-outs).* All strikes not aimed at achieving a collective agreement and not called or endorsed by a trade union are prohibited and employees in the privatised railway and postal services who have retained the status of civil servants are denied the right to strike.

Education

▶ *Article 7§3 – prohibition of children employment under 15.* The mandatory rest period for children still subject to compulsory education during school holidays is not sufficient to ensure that they may benefit from compulsory education.

Movement of persons

▶ *Article 13§4 – right to emergency assistance until repatriation has taken place.* Non-EU or EEA nationals may not claim social assistance if they are not resident in Germany.

▶ *Article 18§2 – right to simplification and liberalisation of formalities related to immigration.* Complex formalities remain in respect of the granting and renewal of work and residence permits.

▶*Article 19§6 – right to family reunion.* 1. The age limit for the entry of children of migrant workers, nationals of Contracting Parties to the Charter who are not covered by Community regulations, for purposes of family reunion is set at 16 years. 2. Family reunion is not allowed to young persons with only one parent residing in Germany, except in special cases. 3. There is no right to family reunion for spouses of second-generation foreigners, unless the latter have been resident in Germany for 8 years and if the marriage has existed for at least one year.

▶*Articles 13§1 and 19§8 - right to guarantees in case of expulsion and repatriation.* Non EU or EEA nationals may be deported under the 1991 Foreign Nationals Act for not being able to meet own needs or those of dependants without recourse to social assistance, for using heroin, cocaine and other drugs, for prolonged homelessness, for recourse to assistance for the upbringing of children outside the family, for serious crime committed by minors.

Equality (nationality)

Discrimination against non EU or EEA nationals in the following matters:

▶ payment of the supplementary child-raising allowance in the Länder of Baden-Württemberg and Bavaria (reserved for German nationals, EU and EEA nationals)

Article 16 - rights of the family (family benefits).

▶ granting of several social assistance benefits under the Federal Social Assistance Act (reserved for German nationals, EU and EEA nationals).

Article 13§1 and §3 – individual right to adequate social and medical assistance, right to advice and to social services.

▶ the employment of persons who are obliged to perform military service is not guaranteed and the length of military service is not treated as equivalent to time worked in an enterprise.

Article 19§4 – right to equal treatment in conditions of employment.

— Greece —

Greece ratified the European Social Charter on 06/06/1984 and Protocol No. 1, which adds new rights, on 18/06/1998. It has accepted 67 of the 72 paragraphs of the Charter and the 4 paragraphs of Protocol No. 1.

Greece ratified Protocol No. 2 reforming the control mechanism on 12/09/1996 and Protocol No. 3 on "collective complaints" on 18/06/1998. It has not yet made a declaration enabling national NGOs to submit complaints.

Greece has signed but not yet ratified the revised Charter.

Between 1986 and 2000, Greece submitted 11 reports on the application of the Social Charter. The next report on the hard core provisions was due on 30/06/2001.

Greece's record with respect to application of the Charter is the following as of 1 July 2001:

Examples of progress achieved or being achieved

Health/Education
▶ The minimum age for admission to employment has been set at 15 years (Act No. 1837/1989). Children employed in family businesses in agriculture, including livestock farming, or forestry now come within the general prohibition on child labour (presidential decree No. 62/1998). *Article 7§§1 and 3 – prohibition of the employment of children under 15.*

Equality (nationality)
▶ Access by nationals of other Contracting Parties to all vocational guidance and training programmes run by the OAED (Act No. 2224/1994). *Articles 9 and 10 – right to vocational guidance and training.*

Employment
▶ Prohibition of dismissal of employees of the merchant navy during pregnancy (presidential decree of 1997). *Article 8§2 – prohibition of dismissal during maternity leave*

Movement of persons
▶ Simplification of the procedures for issuing work permits (Act No. 2910/2001 on the entry of foreign nationals into Greek territory and their

residence therein). Repeal of Section 19 of the Nationality Code, under which Greek nationals leaving the country with no intention of returning could be deprived of their Greek nationality (Act No. 2623/1998). *Article 18 – right to simplification and liberalisation of formalities related to immigration.*

▶ Draft law designed to reduce from 5 to 3 years the period for which nationals of other Contracting Parties not members of the EU or the EEA must wait in order to be reunited with their families. *Article 19§6 – right to family reunion*

Cases of non-compliance

Health
▶ *Article 11§3 – right to preventive measures (regulations and prophylactic measures).* The measures taken to combat smoking are inadequate.

Equality

Sex
▶ *Article 1§2 – Prohibition of discrimination in employment.* The law limits the number of women who may be admitted to police training; this is effectively a form of discrimination against women.

Nationality
Discrimination against nationals of other Contracting Parties not members of the EU or the EEA with regard to:
▶ the payment of family benefit (residence requirement for children).
Articles 12§4 and 16 – right to equal treatment with respect to family benefit.

Employment
▶ *Article 1§2 – prohibition of forced labour.* 1. The civilian population may be mobilised in any "unforeseen situation causing disruption of the country's economy and society." 2. Career army officers who have received certain kinds of training may be denied permission to leave the army for up to twenty-five years. 3. Criminal sanctions can be imposed on seafarers in cases where neither the safety of the vessel nor the lives or health of those on board are in danger.

▶ *Article 1§3 – right to free employment services.* The performance of the public employment services is patently unsatisfactory.

▶ *Article 4§4 – right to notice of termination of employment.* The notice periods are insufficient for workers with less than 10 years' service.

Social Protection

▶ *Article 13§1 – individual right to adequate social and medical assistance.* The laws on social assistance allow the authorities a wide measure of discretion, undermining the effectiveness of judicial review.

Movement of persons

▶ *Article 18§§2 and 3 – right to simplification and liberalisation of formalities related to immigration..* 1. No measures taken to relax the procedures for issuing work permits to nationals of states not members of the EU or the EEA. 2. Obligation on foreign nationals to leave Greek territory if they lose their jobs.

▶ *Article 19§6 – right to family reunion.* Nationals of other Contracting Parties not members of the EU or the EEA must wait 5 years before applying for family reunion.

▶ *Article 19§8 – right to guarantees in the event of expulsion.* The grounds for expulsion set out in Section 27 of Act No. 1975/1991 (prison sentence, or if the presence of the individual concerned poses a threat to public health) go beyond those permitted by the Charter.

— Hungary —

Hungary ratified the European Social Charter on 08/07/1999. Hungary has accepted 33 of the Charter's 72 paragraphs.

Hungary has signed but not yet ratified Protocol No. 2 reforming the control mechanism.

Hungary has neither signed nor ratified Protocol No. 1 which adds new rights, Protocol No. 3 on "collective complaints" and the revised Charter.

The first report on all the accepted provisions of the Charter is due on 31/03/2002.

– Iceland –

Iceland ratified the European Social Charter on 15/01/1976. Iceland has accepted 41 of the Charter's 72 paragraphs.

Iceland has signed but not yet ratified Protocol No. 1 which adds new rights and the revised Charter.

Iceland has neither signed nor ratified Protocol No. 2 reforming the control mechanism and Protocol No. 3 on "collective complaints".

Between 1981 and 2000 Iceland has submitted 14 reports on the application of the Charter. Iceland submitted its 15th report on the hard core provisions of the Charter on 23/10/2001.

Iceland's record with respect to application of the Charter is the following as of 1 July 2001:

Examples of progress achieved or being achieved

Employment

▶ Article 180 of the Criminal Code which provided for imprisonment if a person became a public burden, neglected his maintenance obligations and refused to take on a job was repealed (Act of 14 June 1985). Section 81 of the Seamen's Act which provided for criminal sanctions against a crew member rising against the shipmaster even if not using the force, was repealed (Act of 4 May 1990). *Article 1§2 – prohibition of forced labour*

Right to organise

▶ The requirement that taxi drivers have to belong to a specified trade union in order to operate was abolished (Act No. 61/1995). The Constitution was amended to expressly recognise the negative right to organise (Act No. 97/1995). *Article 5 - right to organise*

Cases of non-compliance

Employment / Right to organise

▶ *Article 2§1 – right to reasonable working hours.* In the absence of a reasonable time limit on overtime daily working hours may in certain cases be up to sixteen hours and since weekly working hours may also be excessive.

▶ *Article 5 - right to organise.* The Government has not shown that the Constitution - although amended - amounts to a protection of the negative freedom of association of a scope large enough to avoid in practice an obligation to belong to a trade union being imposed by closed shop or priority clauses in collective agreements.

▶ *Article 6§4 - right to collective bargaining (strikes and lock-outs).* The right of civil servants to strike is limited to situations in which the strike is aimed at the conclusion of a collective agreement.

Movement of persons

▶ *Article 18§3 – right to simplification and liberalisation of formalities related to immigration.* Repeated lack of information.

Equality (nationality)

Discrimination against non EU or EEA nationals in the following matters:

▶ Granting of family allowances (subject to a residence requirement of children).

Articles 12§4 and 16 – right to equal treatment with respect to family benefits.

▶ No accumulation of periods of insurance or employment.

Article 12§4 – right to equal treatment in social security matters.

▶ Entitlement to medical assistance (subject to a 6 months residence requirement).

Article 13§1 – individual right to adequate social and medical assistance.

– Ireland –

Ireland ratified the European Social Charter on 07/10/1964 and the revised Charter on 04/11/2000. Ireland accepted 63 of the 72 paragraphs of the Charter and 92 of the 98 paragraphs of the revised Charter.

Ireland ratified Protocol No. 2 reforming the control mechanism on 14/05/1997 and Protocol No. 3 on "collective complaints" on 04/11/2000. It has not yet made a declaration enabling national NGOs to submit collective complaints.

Between 1966 and 2000, Ireland submitted 19 reports on the application of the Social Charter. The next report on the hard core provisions of the Social Charter was due on 30/06/2001.

Ireland's record with respect to application of the Charter is the following as of 1 July 2001:

Examples of progress achieved or being achieved

Employment/right to organise
▶ Repeal of the 1894 law on merchant shipping which provided for criminal sanctions for seamen not returning to ship or not carrying out orders (1998 Merchant Shipping Act) *Article 1§2 – prohibition of forced labour*
▶ Introduction of a statutory minimum wage (2000 Act on the National Minimum Wage). *Article 4§1 – right to a fair remuneration.*
▶ Bill repealing section 9 of the 1939 Offences Against the State Act, which allows the prosecution of public service officials and employees for taking strike action *Article 6§4 – right to collective bargaining (strikes and lock-outs)*

Education
▶ Time spent by young people and teenagers in vocational training has been included in normal working hours (1977 Protection of Young Persons (Employment) Act) *Article 7§6 – right of young people between 15 and 18 to special working conditions (time for training)*
▶ The Protection of Young Persons (Employment) Act, 1996 sets out a broader definition of a child for the purpose of employment by including all persons under the age of 16 years or, if higher, still subject to compulsory schooling. The limits on working time for children aged 14 and 15 are set at 7

hours per day and 35 hours per week. *Article 7§3 – prohibition of employment of children under 15 years.*

Equality

Sex
▶ Repeal of measures discriminating against the employment of women in the civil service *Article 1§2 – prohibition of discrimination in employment*

Property
▶ Elimination of discrimination against persons receiving social and medical assistance (changes to the 1972 local elections act and the appendix to the 1898 decree on local authorities) *Article 13§2 – non-discrimination in respect of social and political rights*

Birth
▶ Elimination of discrimination against children born out of wedlock in respect of custody, and the right of ownership and succession (1987 Status of Children Act) *Article 17 – rights of young persons (legal and social protection)*

Social protection
▶ The courts are competent to rule on divorce (1996 Family Law (Divorce) Act *Article 16 – rights of family (legal protection)*
▶ The Government has adopted a 10 year plan for the fight against poverty (National Anti-Poverty Strategy – NAPS), the target of which is to reduce the number of people in consistent poverty to less than 5% by 2004. *Article 13§1 – individual right to adequate assistance.*

Cases of non-compliance

Movement of persons
▶ The power of the Minister of the Interior to issue expulsion orders has been restricted in that he must take account of the age, family status, employment prospects and length of stay of the person concerned (1999 Immigration Act) *Article 16 – rights of family (legal protection)*

Health
▶ *Article 8§1 – right to maternity leave.* A post-natal maternity leave of at least six weeks is not guaranteed in law.
▶ *Article 8§4 – prohibition of employment of women in certain dangerous types of work.* Legislation does not prohibit the employment of women in underground extraction work and in mines.

Health/Education

▶ *Article 7§3 – prohibition of employment of children under 15.* The mandatory rest period during school holidays for children still subject to compulsory school is not sufficient to ensure that they may benefit from such education and children employed by a close relative are not afforded the protection required.

Employment

▶ *Article 1§2 - prohibition of forced labour* The period of compulsory service required from officers is excessive since a tender of resignation may be refused at the discretion of the Minister of Defence.

▶ *Article 2§1 – reasonable working hours* 1. Legislation on working hours permits a 60-hour working week, overtime included. 2. Legislation covering hotel staff permits a working week of up to 66 hours, overtime included. 3. Legislation on working hours does not apply to certain categories, such as office workers, sales representatives and the self-employed.

▶ *Article 2§4 - reduced working hours or additional holidays for workers in dangerous or unhealthy occupations* No provision is made for reduced working hours or additional holidays in dangerous or unhealthy occupations.

▶ *Article 4§1 – adequate remuneration* During the period 1994-1996, 6.5% of the workforce received an inadequate gross wage (less than 2.50 IEP per hour, ie less than 51% of average net wages in manufacturing). Low gross hourly wages were paid in 1997 to general ancillary workers in the retail grocery sector.

▶ *Article 4§4 – reasonable notice of termination of employment* 1. The minimum statutory notice periods provided for in law (ranging from 1 to 8 weeks) are not adequate. 2. Established civil servants do not receive a notice period but instead a 14-day period during which the person concerned may make representations against a proposed dismissal.

▶ *Article 7§5 – right of young persons between 15 and 18 years old to special working conditions (remuneration).* The wage differences in the labour market are excessive: a young worker earns on average only about 40% of the starting wage of an adult and adult wages are not considered adequate.

Social protection

▶ *Article 13§1 – individual right to social and medical adequate assistance.* Medical assistance, via a medical card, is subject to a requirement of "ordinary" residence of one year in the state.

Right to organise

▶ *Article 5 - right to organise* 1. Clauses allowing trade union monopoly exist - The right not to join a trade union is inadequately protected in law and in practice. 2. Members of non-authorised trade unions are not protected against dismissals based on their membership or union activities by the 1973 Unfair Dismissals Act (as amended).

▶ *Articles 5 and 6§2 - right to organise and right to collective bargaining* The conditions laid down for the granting of a negotiation licence are too strict.

▶ *Article 6§4 - right to collective bargaining (strikes and lock-outs)* Only authorised trade unions (ie. those holding a negotiation licence) and their members are afforded immunity against civil action in the event of a strike and, under the Unfair Dismissals Act, an employer may dismiss all employees for taking part in strike action.

Equality (nationality)

▶ Discrimination against foreign nationals non EU or EEA nationals in the following matter: granting of family allowances (subject to a condition of residence of the children).

Articles 12§4 and 16 - equal treatment with respect to family benefits

export of benefits granted under Irish legislation in case of occupational accidents or disease and the accumulation of insurance or employment periods (not guaranteed).

Article 12§4 right to social security

▶ Adequate means of appeal to an independent court against a deportation order are not available to nationals of Contracting Parties to the Charter which are not members of the EU or party to the 1955 Convention on Establishment..

Article 19§8 – right to guarantees in case of expulsion .

Movement of persons

▶ *Article 18§3 – Right to simplification and liberalisation of formalities related to immigration.* Existing regulations have not be liberalised.

▶ *Article 19§6 – right to family reunion* The official age limit for family reunion is under 21 years of age, and the Government has failed to provide any figures proving that children between the ages of 18 and 21 are able in practice to join their parents.

— Italy —

Italy ratified the European Social Charter on 22/10/1965 and the revised Charter on 05/07/1999. It has accepted the 72 paragraphs of the Charter and 97 of the 98 paragraphs of the revised Charter.

Italy ratified Protocol No. 3 on "collective complaints" on 03/11/1997. It has not yet made a declaration enabling national NGOs to submit collective complaints.

Between 1967 and 2000, Italy submitted 20 reports on the application of the Social Charter. The first report on the hard core provisions of the revised Charter was due on 30/06/2001.

Italy's record with respect to application of the Charter is the following as of 1 July 2001:

Examples of progress achieved or being achieved

Health
▶ Prohibition of night work by women between midnight and 6 am from confirmation of pregnancy until the child's first birthday. Female wage earners with a child under 3 years of age cannot be required to perform night work, nor may wage earners of either sex with a disabled dependant (Act of 5 February 1999). *Article 8§4 – regulation of night work.*
▶ Prohibition on assigning pregnant women or nursing mothers to work in which they are exposed to ionising radiation, lead or derivatives thereof (Legislative Decree No. 645/1996). *Article 8§4 – prohibition of the employment of women in certain dangerous types of work.*

Health/Education
▶ Prohibition of the employment of children under the age of 15 in all sectors of the economy – Minors may only be employed in hazardous work for the purpose of vocational training, under the supervision of a competent instructor and only for the time necessary (Legislative Decree No. 345/1999). *Article 7§1 and 2 – Prohibition of the employment of children under the age of 15.*

Social Protection
▶ Introduction of a minimum integration income for a trial period of two years (1999-2000) (Legislative Decree No. 237 of 18 June 1998). Draft law as amended reorganising social assistance benefits (No. 4931 passed on

18 October 2000) sets out the "right" to assistance for anyone residing in Italy. *Article 13§1 – individual right to adequate social and medical assistance.*

Equality

▶ Repeal of Section 13 of Act No. 943 of 30 December 1986 whereby a 0.5% tax was deducted from the pay of nationals of Contracting Parties not members of the EU. *Article 19§5 – right to equal treatment in respect of taxes and dues.*

Employment

▶ Prohibition on dismissing domestic employees during the compulsory period of maternity leave (national collective agreement on domestic employment of 16 July 1996) – Female domestic employees who do not qualify for maternity benefit are entitled to "maternity cheques" (Act No. 448/1998). *Article 8§2 – prohibition of dismissal during maternity leave.*

Movement of Persons

▶ Liberalisation of the rules governing the employment of foreign nationals (Legislative Decree No. 286/1998). *Article 18§3 – right to simplification and liberalisation of formalities related to immigration.*

▶ Prohibition of expulsion on the ground of destitution. *Article 19§8 – right to guarantees in the event of expulsion.*

Cases of non-compliance

Health

▶ *Article 3§1 – right to health and safety at work (regulations).* Italy has failed to demonstrate compliance with this requirement, in that self-employed workers in agriculture, trade and industry and members of their families working with them are not always covered by occupational health and safety regulations.

▶ *Article 8§4 – prohibition of the employment of women in certain dangerous types of work.* There is no prohibition on employing women in underground mining.

▶ *Article 2§4 – right to compensatory time off in dangerous occupations.* There are no arrangements for reducing working hours or granting additional holidays for workers in dangerous or unhealthy occupations.

▶ *Article 7§2 – prohibition of the employment of children under the age of 15.* The age limit for admission to employment involving contact with benzene is 16 years.

Health/Education

▶ *Article 7§1 – prohibition of the employment of children under the age of 15.* The employment of children under 15 is not prohibited in agriculture or domestic work.

▶ *Article 7§3 – prohibition of the employment of children under the age of 15.* National law on the minimum age of admission to employment is not observed in practice.

▶ *Article 7§4 – right of young people between 15 and 18 to special working conditions (working time)*. The Italian government has not demonstrated that the majority of young people under the age of 16 are entitled, under legislation or collective agreements, to a limitation of working hours.

Employment

▶ *Article 1§2 – prohibition of forced labour.* 1. The Shipping Code provides for criminal sanctions against seafarers and civil aviation personnel who desert their post or refuse to obey orders, even in cases where neither the safety of the vessel or aircraft nor the lives or health of those on board are in danger. 2. Act No. 146/1990 governing strikes in essential services exceeds the terms of Article 31 of the Charter.

▶ *Article 4§4 – Reasonable notice of termination of employment.* In certain sectors (particularly the food industry) the periods of notice are unacceptably short (2 days in the case of a worker with at least 2 years' service).

▶ *Article 4§5 – right to limitation of deduction from wages.* Deductions from wages for workers' debts to their employers are not subject to any regulations and are left to the discretion of the competent courts.

▶ *Article 8§3 – right to time off for nursing mothers.* 1. Breastfeeding time during work at home is unpaid. 2. Domestic employees are not entitled to breastfeeding breaks, nor are they paid for any such breaks.

Social Protection

▶ *Article 13§1 – individual right to social and medical adequate assistance.* An individual right to social assistance is not guaranteed in all regions.

Movement of Persons

▶ *Article 19§6 – right to family reunion.* The Italian government has not demonstrated that young people between the ages of 18 and 21 benefit in practice from family reunion.

Equality (nationality)

▶ *Articles 12§4 and 16 – right to equal treatment with respect to family benefit.* The payment of family benefit to nationals of other Contracting Parties not members of the EU or the EEA is subject to the children concerned being resident in Italy.

– Lithuania –

Lithuania ratified the revised European Social Charter on 29/06/2001. Lithuania has accepted 86 of the revised Charter's 98 paragraphs.

Lithuania has not agreed to be bound by the "collective complaints" procedure.

The first report on the hard core provisions of the revised Charter is due on 30/06/2003.

— Luxembourg —

Luxembourg ratified the European Social Charter on 10/10/1991. Luxembourg has accepted all of the Charter's 72 paragraphs.

Luxembourg has signed but not yet ratified the revised Charter, Protocol No. 1 which adds new rights or Protocol No. 2 reforming the control mechanism. Luxembourg has not signed or ratified Protocol No. 3 on "collective complaints".

Between 1993 et 2000, Luxembourg submitted 4 reports on the application of the Charter. The next report on the hard core provisions was due on 30/06/2001.

Luxembourg's record with respect to application of the Charter is the following as of 1 July 2001:

Examples of progress achieved or being achieved

Social Protection
▶ The minimum age requirement for entitlement to the guaranteed minimum wage has been lowered to 25 years and the condition of residence reduced to 5 years (Act of 29 April 2000). *Article 13§1 – individual right to adequate social and medical assistance.*

Employment
▶ The deductions made to the wages of young workers aged between 15 and 16 have been reviewed in accordance with the deductions allowed by the Charter (Act of 22 December 2000). *Article 7§5 – right of young people between 15 and 18 to special working conditions (remuneration).*
▶ It is now forbidden to give a woman notice of dismissal during maternity leave and a woman unlawfully dismissed may now request that her dismissal be annulled and that she be maintained in her job (Act of 7 July 1998). *Article 8§2 – prohibition of dismissal during maternity leave.*

Cases of non-compliance

Health

▶ *Article 2§4 – right to compensatory time off in dangerous occupations.* There is no system for reducing working time or giving additional paid leave to those employed in dangerous or unhealthy occupations.

▶ *Article 7§4 – right of young people between 15 and 18 to special working conditions (working time).* Working time for young people under 16 (up to 8 hours per day and 40 hours per week) is excessive.

Movement of persons

▶ *Article 19§8 – right to guarantees in case of expulsion.* The grounds for expulsion provided by the amended Act of 28 March 1972 on the entry and stay of foreign nationals, their medical examination and employment go beyond those permitted by the Charter.

Equality (nationality)

Discrimination against non EU or EEA nationals in the following matters:

▶ Granting of family allowances (subject to a children's residence requirement).

Articles 12§4 and 16 – right to equal treatment with respect to family benefits.

▶ Eligibility for election to joint works councils.

Articles 5 and 19§4 – right to equal treatment in trade union matters.

▶ *Article 19§7 – right to equal treatment in respect of legal proceedings.* Nationals of States that have not ratified the 1954 Hague Convention on Civil Procedure are obliged to lodge a security when applied for by the defendant and agreed to by the court.

Employment

▶ *Article 4§2 – right to increased remuneration for overtime.* After the ninth hour of overtime, State officials and employees are not entitled to an increased compulsory rest period or to increased remuneration if the overtime was performed between 6 and 10 p.m. or not during the week-end or public holidays.

— Malta —

Malta ratified the European Social Charter on 04/10/1988. Malta has accepted 55 of the 72 paragraphs of the Charter.

Malta ratified Protocol No. 2 reforming the control mechanism on 16/02/1994.

Malta has not signed or ratified Protocol No. 1, which adds new rights, the revised Charter or Protocol No. 3 on "collective complaints".

Between 1990 and 2000, Malta submitted 8 reports on the application of the Social Charter. The 9th report on the hard core provisions was submitted on 26/07/2001.

Malta's record with respect to application of the Charter is the following as of 1 July 2001:

Examples of progress achieved or being achieved

Health
▶ The regulations on the medical supervision of young workers apply to all workers in all sectors (1994 Act on the promotion of health and safety at work). *Article 7§9 – right of young people between 15 and 18 to special working conditions (medical control).*
▶ The right to maternity leave has been extended to part-time employees (1996 regulation). *Article 8§1 – right to maternity leave.*
▶ Prohibition on assigning an employee while she is pregnant, following delivery or while she is breastfeeding to work which may pose hazards for the course of her pregnancy or her own or the child's physical and mental health (administrative regulation 92/2000). *Article 8§4 – prohibition of the employment of women in certain dangerous types of work.*

Equality

Sex
▶ Elimination of gender-based discrimination with regard to the payment of survivor's pension and sickness benefit (changes made with effect from 1 January 1998). *Article 12§1 – right to social security.*
▶ Elimination of discrimination between spouses in wedlock and with regard to children including replacement of paternal responsibility by parental authority (Act No. XXI of 1993). *Article 16 – rights of the family (legal protection).*

Nationality
▶ Entitlement to the social security benefits provided for in the Social Security Act of 1987 has been extended to include nationals of other Contracting Parties (European Social Charter Order, 1999). *Articles 13 and 16 – right to social assistance and family rights (family benefit).*

Employment
▶ A bill containing new provisions in favour of Malta's police force was tabled before Parliament in 1998. *Article 5 – the right to organise.*

Cases of non-compliance

Health/Education
▶ *Article 7§3 – prohibition of the employment of children.* The restriction on the number of hours that may be worked on a school day (4 hours) by young persons subject to compulsory education is insufficient to ensure that these children enjoy the full benefit of that education.

Health
▶ *Article 8§1 – right to maternity leave.* 1. Six-week postnatal leave is not compulsory. 2. Female employees who do not give their employer three weeks' notice prior to the commencement of maternity leave are entitled to only five weeks' leave beginning on the date of confinement. 3. Employees who are related to the employer do not have the same rights as other employees with regard to maternity leave.

Social Protection
▶ *Article 8§1 – right to maternity benefit.* 1. The social security benefits for female employees not entitled to the maternity allowance are inadequate. 2. Employees who decide not to return to work after maternity leave are required to pay back their maternity allowances.

Employment
▶ *Article 2§3 – right to annual holiday with pay.* Employees can waive their right to annual leave in return for additional pay.
▶ *Article 2§5 – right to weekly rest.* Workers required to work on their weekly rest day are not entitled to time off *in lieu.*
▶ *Article 4§4 – right to notice of termination of employment.* Certain periods of notice are unacceptably short (1 week for workers with up to one year of service; 2 weeks for workers in their second year of service; 8 weeks for workers with more than 5 years' service).

▶ *Article 8§2 – prohibition of dismissal during maternity leave.* Certain categories of employees (employees who are related to the employer, part-time employees) are not protected against dismissal during maternity leave.

Equality

Nationality
▶ *Article 8§1 – right to maternity benefit.* Save where there is a bilateral agreement, employees who are nationals of other Contracting Parties are not entitled to the maternity benefit provided for in the 1952 Act.

▶ *Article 13§1 – individual right to adequate assistance.* The disability pension, the pension for the visually impaired and the old-age pension are reserved exclusively for Maltese nationals (Sections 27 and 66 of the Social Security Act of 1987). Nationals of other Contracting Parties which have not ratified the European Convention on Social and Medical Assistance (1953) are not entitled to the social or medical assistance benefits provided for in Sections 19 and 30 of the 1987 Act.

Birth
▶ *Article 17 – rights of young persons (legal and social protection).* 1. Children born out of wedlock are discriminated against in matters of succession. 2. Inequalities exist between children of a first and second marriage.

Right to organise
▶ *Articles 5, 6§2 and §3 – right to organise and right to bargain collectively.* Possibility for one of the parties to a collective dispute to ask the minister to refer the matter to compulsory arbitration.

▶ *Articles 5 and 6§2 – right to organise and right to bargain collectively.* Restrictions on trade union rights in the Maltese police force (compulsory membership of an occupational organisation with limited powers).

▶ *Article 6§4 – right to bargain collectively (strikes and lock-outs).* The Maltese government has repeatedly failed to show that this right is respected.

Movement of persons
▶ *Article 13§4 – right to emergency assistance pending repatriation.* Nationals of other Contracting Parties which have not ratified the European Convention on Social and Medical Assistance (1953) are not entitled to any social assistance.

— Moldova —

Moldova ratified the revised European Social Charter on 08/11/2001 and has accepted 60 of the revised Charter's 98 paragraphs.

Moldova has not agreed to be bound by the "collective complaints" procedure.

The first report, on the hard core provisions of the revised Charter, is due on 31/03/2004.

— The Netherlands —

The Netherlands ratified the European Social Charter on 22/04/1980 and Protocol No. 1 which adds new rights on 05/08/1992. The Netherlands has accepted all of the Charter's 72 paragraphs[1] and 3 of the 4 provisions of Protocol No. 1. As regards the Netherlands Antilles and Aruba, the Netherlands has accepted 10 paragraphs.

The Netherlands ratified Protocol No. 2 reforming the control mechanism on 01/06/1991. The Netherlands has not signed or ratified the revised Charter or Protocol No. 3 on "collective complaints".

Between 1982 and 2000 the Netherlands submitted 13 reports on the application of the Charter. The 14th report on the hard core provisions of the Charter was submitted on 10/09/2001. As regards the Netherlands Antilles and Aruba 6 reports have been submitted.

The Netherlands's record with respect to application of the Charter is the following as of 1 July 2001:

Examples of progress made or under way

Health
▶ Extension of maternity leave from 12 to 16 weeks (Act of 22 February 1990). *Article 8§1 – right to maternity leave.*

Equality

Sex
▶ Adoption in 1994 of a general Act on equal treatment covering all forms of discrimination – The prohibition of discrimination between men and women was extended to categories of persons eligible for pensions, to pension rules and the implementation of pensions schemes (WGB amended in 1998). *Articles 1§2 and Prot. No. 1 – right to equal treatment and opportunities in employment.*
▶ Prohibition of dismissing an employee because he has brought legal or extra judicial proceedings to obtain equal remuneration (Act on "reparation" of 1989). *Article 4§3 – right to equal pay.*

---

[1] Where the Netherlands Antilles and Aruba are concerned, the Netherlands are bound by Articles 1, 5, 6 and 16 of the Charter.

▶Unmarried parents may exercise joint parental authority – Joint parental authority is maintained even if the parents separate (Civil Code amended in 1995 and 1998). *Article 16 – rights of the family (legal protection).*

Employment/Right to organise

▶ Repeal of Article 6 of the Exceptional Decree of 1945 on professional relations pursuant to which a worker had to obtain authorisation in order to terminate his employment (Act on Flexibility and Security of 1999). *Article 1§2 – prohibition of forced labour.*

▶Reduction from 100 to 50 employees of the threshold from which a works council must be created in the workplace (WOR amended in 1998) – Employees and workers, national insurance and subsidised institutions are authorised freely to conclude collective agreements on their conditions of employment (Repeal in 1995 of the WAGGS). *Article 6§1 – right to collective bargaining (joint consultation).*

Social Protection

▶ Domestic workers and women working in public health for less than three days per week are entitled to maternity leave and benefits (Act of 2000) *Article 8§1 – right to maternity leave and benefits.*

Movement of persons

▶ Migrant workers are entitled to be treated no less favourably than nationals as regards legal proceedings (Law of 8 March 1980). *Article 19§7 – right to equal treatment in respect of legal proceedings.*

Cases of non-compliance

The Netherlands (Kingdom in Europe)

Health

▶*Article 2§4 – right to compensatory time off in dangerous occupations.* There is no system of reduced working time or additional paid leave for dangerous or unhealthy occupations

▶*Article 3§1 – right to health and safety at work.* Self-employed workers do not appear to have satisfactory protection as regards health and safety at work.

Education

▶*Article 7§3 – prohibition of employment of children under 15.* 1. Children aged 15 who are subject to compulsory school attendance may work as deliverers from 6 a.m. for up to 2 hours per day 5 days a week before school. 2. The legal rest period provided in the school holidays for children of compulsory school age is not sufficient to guarantee them the full benefit of compulsory instruction.

▶ *Article 7§6 – right of young people between 15 and 18 to special working conditions (time for vocational training).* The Netherlands government has not shown that the great majority of young workers, and in particular apprentices, have the right to treat time spent on vocational training as normal working hours.

Social Protection

▶ *Article 12§3 – right to social security (improvement and safeguard).* The evolution of the social security system in the sickness and invalidity sectors calls in question the collective nature of the financing of the benefits paid out in those sectors.

Employment

▶*Article 2§1 – right to reasonable working time.* The provisions governing the introduction of measures for flexibility in working time do not safeguard collective bargaining sufficiently to protect workers and consequently, the maximum length of the working week provided in the context of the "rules on flexibility" cannot be considered as reasonable.

▶ *Article 4§1 – right to a fair remuneration.* The minimum wage for workers aged under 23 years constitutes a percentage of the minimum wage for adults which is too far below the average national income.

▶ *Article 7§5 – right of young people between 15 and 18 to special working conditions (remuneration).* The reductions applied to the minimum wage for apprentices are excessive in relation to the minimum wage for adult workers.

▶ *Article 4§4 – right to notice of dismissal.* All workers, in particular minors, are not guaranteed an appropriate period of notice of dismissal.

Movement of persons

▶*Article 18§3 – right to simplification and liberalisation of formalities related to immigration.* There is no sign of increased flexibility in the rules governing the conditions placed on access to the employment market for non-EU nationals.

▶*Article 19§6 – right to family reunion.* Excessive restrictions are placed on family reunion in the case of nationals of certain States (age of children and waiting period).

The Netherlands Antilles and Aruba

Employment

▶ *Article 5 – right to organise.* Equal treatment for foreign trade union representatives is not secured as regards their eligibility to be elected to an official body in which the social partners participate.

Social Protection/Housing

▶ *Article 16 – rights of family.* Lack of information about essential questions concerning the implementation of social, legal and economic protection for the family.

— Norway —

Norway ratified the European Social Charter on 26/10/1962 and the revised Charter on 07/05/2001. It has accepted 60 of the 72 paragraphs of the Charter and 79 of the 98 paragraphs of the revised Charter.

Norway ratified Protocol No. 3 on "collective complaints" on 20/03/1997. It has not yet made a declaration enabling national NGOs to submit complaints.

Between 1964 and 2000, Norway submitted 20 reports on the application of the Social Charter. The 21st report on the hard core provisions of the Charter was submitted on 20/08/2001.

Norway's record with respect to application of the Charter is the following as of 1 July 2001:

Examples of progress achieved and being achieved

Employment

▶ Repeal of the Seafarers Act of 17 July 1953, which allowed criminal sanctions to be imposed on seafarers who deserted their post or committed disciplinary offences even in cases where neither the safety of the vessel nor the lives or health of those on board were in danger (Act of 30 May 1975). Abolition of compulsory service for dentists. *Article 1§2 – prohibition of forced labour.*

Movement of persons

▶ Extension of the scope of family reunion to include children only one of whose parents is living in Norway (1991 immigration directives, as amended in 1997). *Article 19§6 – right to family reunion.*

Cases of non-compliance

Education/Health

▶ *Article 7§3 – prohibition of the employment of children under the age of 15.* The mandatory rest period during school holidays for children still subject to compulsory education is not sufficient to ensure that they benefit from such education.

Social Protection

▶   *Article 12§3 – right to social security (improvement and safeguard).* The changes made to the rules governing the payment of unemployment benefit are too restrictive and not commensurate with the objectives pursued.

Employment

▶   *Article 2§1 – right to reasonable working hours.* The total number of working hours in any twenty-four-hour period may in certain circumstances exceed sixteen hours.

Right to organise

▶   *Article 6§3 – right to bargain collectively (conciliation and arbitration).* During the reference period, arbitration was imposed which went beyond the circumstances provided for in Article 31 of the Charter.

▶   *Article 6§4 – right to bargain collectively (strikes and lock-outs).* 1. The obligation to keep the peace in the state sector is too general. 2. The Norwegian Parliament has introduced legislation to terminate industrial action and impose arbitration in circumstances which go beyond those permitted by Article 31 of the Charter.

Equality (nationality)

Discrimination against nationals of other Contracting Parties not members of the EU or the EEA in the following matters:

▶   the payment of family benefit (residence requirement for children). *Articles 12§4 and 16 – right to equal treatment with respect to family benefit.*

▶ the aggregation of periods of insurance or employment (no provision to this effect).

Article 12§4 – right to social security.

▶ the granting of social assistance (permanent residence requirement).

Article 13§1 – individual right to adequate social and medical assistance.

▶ No guarantee that discrimination will not occur in practice with regard to the allocation of low-cost housing by municipal authorities (length of residence requirement).

Article 19§4 – right to equal treatment with regard to access to housing.

— Poland —

Poland ratified the European Social Charter on 25/06/1997. Poland has accepted 58 of the Charter's 72 paragraphs.

Poland ratified Protocol No. 2 reforming the control mechanism on 25/06/1997. Poland has not signed or ratified Protocol No. 1 which adds new rights, Protocol No. 3 on "collective complaints" or the revised Charter.

In 1999, Poland submitted its first report on the application of the Charter. The 2nd report on the hard core provisions was submitted on 22/10/2001.

The Poland's record with respect to application of the Charter is the following as of 1 July 2001:

Cases of non-compliance

Employment

▶ *Article 4§2 – right to increased remuneration for overtime* Employees who have worked overtime are entitled to an hourly compensation equivalent to the additional hours worked. They are not entitled to increased remuneration.

▶ *Article 4§4 – right to notice of dismissal.* The Labour Code provides that two-weeks notice must be given to terminate a fixed-term contract of more than six months, which does not constitute reasonable notice.

— Portugal —

Portugal ratified the European Social Charter on 30/09/1991. It has accepted all of the Charter's 72 paragraphs;

Portugal ratified Protocol No. 1 reforming the control mechanism on 08/03/1993. It ratified Protocol No. 3 on "collective complaints" on 20/03/1998. It has not yet made a declaration enabling national NGOs to submit complaints.

Portugal has signed, but not yet ratified, the revised Charter.

Between 1993 and 2000, Portugal submitted 6 reports on the application of the Social Charter. The 7th report on the hard core provisions was submitted on 10/10/2001.

Portugal's record with respect to application of the Charter is the following as of 1 July 2001:

Examples of progress made or under way

Health/Education

▶ Prohibition of the employment of minors subject to compulsory education (Constitutional Act No. 1/97); the minimum age for employment has been fixed as 16 and light work has been defined (Act No. 58/99); illegal employment of young persons is regarded a very serious offence and sanctions have been stepped up (Acts Nos. 113, 114, 116 and 118/1999). *Article 7§1 – Prohibition of the employment of young people under 15 years of age.*

▶ General prohibition of night work between 8 p.m. and 7 a.m. for young persons under 16 years of age and between 11 p.m. and 7 a.m. for young persons over 16 years of age has been introduced (Act No 58/99). *Article 7§8 – Prohibition of night work for young persons between 15 and 18 years of age.*

▶ Six-weeks post-natal leave has been made compulsory (Act No. 142/99 of 31 August 1999) and maternity leave has been increased from 98 to 120 days (Act No. 18/98 of 28 April 1998). *Article 8§1 – Right to maternity leave and benefits.*

▶ The right to time off for nursing mothers has been extended to cover the whole period of nursing, including in the case of part-time work (Act No. 142/99). *Article 8§3 – Right to time off for nursing mothers.*

Employment/Right to organise

▶ Articles 132 and 133 of the Criminal and Disciplinary Code of the Merchant Navy, which provided for sanctions for seamen who abandoned their post, have been partly repealed on grounds of their being unconstitutional. *Article 1§2 – Prohibition of forced labour*

▶ The Government has stopped defining by decree the minimum services to be guaranteed in the event of a strike where the parties are unable to reach agreement (decision of the Constitutional Court declaring that certain provisions of the Act on the right to strike were unconstitutional). *Article 6§4 – right to collective bargaining (strikes and lock-outs).*

Movement of persons/Equality

▶ Simplification of the formalities for issuing work permits (Act No. 20/98). *Article 18§1 – right to simplification and liberalisation of formalities related to immigration.*

▶ The scope of the provisions relating to family reunion has been extended (Decree-Law of 8 August 1998). *Article 19§6 – right of foreign nationals to family reunion.*

▶ Abolition of the quota of foreign nationals allowed to work in undertakings with more than five employees (Act No. 20/98). *Articles 18§2 and 19§4 – right to engage in a gainful occupation and right of resident migrants to equal treatment in respect of working conditions.*

▶ Bill to repeal the Decree-Law of 11 August 1977 which gave nationals alone the right to apply for subsidised housing. *Article 19§4 – right to equal treatment in respect of housing.*

Social Protection

▶ Establishment of a guaranteed minimum income (Act No. 19-A/96 of 29 June 1996). *Article 13§1 – individual right to adequate assistance.*

Cases of non-compliance

Health

▶ *Article 3§2 – right to health and safety at work (regulations).* The effective exercise of the right to health and safety at work is not guaranteed given the particularly high number of accidents at work and fatal accidents and the very low number of workplace inspections.

Equality (nationality)

▶ *Article 12§4 – right to social security.* Maltese nationals do not have access to the national health service.

▶ *Article 19§4 - right to equal treatment in respect of housing.* Under the law, access to subsidised housing is limited to Portuguese nationals.

▶ *Article 19§7 – right to equal treatment in respect of legal proceedings.* Foreign nationals must fulfil a condition of 1 year's residence in order to be entitled to legal aid.

Education/Health

▶ *Article 7§1 – prohibition of employment of children under 15 years.* Complaint 1/1998 – International Commission of Jurists v. Portugal (decision of 9 September 1999). Failure to comply in practice with the national legislative provisions on the minimum age for employment.

Employment/Right to organise

▶ *Article 1§2 – prohibition of forced labour.* Articles 132 and 133 of the Criminal and Disciplinary Code for the Merchant Navy of 20 November 1943 provide for sanctions against seamen who abandon their post even where the safety of the vessel or the lives or health of persons on board are not at risk.

▶ *Article 2§2 - right to public holidays with pay.* Employees of undertakings with more than ten employees who have to work on public holidays are not entitled to a compensatory rest period equal to at least the whole of the hours worked.

▶ *Article 13§4 right to assistance.* Social assistance is available to foreign nationals present on Portuguese territory without being resident only if local resources permit.

— Romania —

Romania ratified the revised European Social Charter on 07/05/1999 and has accepted 66 of the revised Charter's 98 paragraphs.

Romania has not agreed to be bound by the "collective complaints" procedure.

The first report on the hard core provisions of the revised Charter was submitted on 18/07/2001.

— Slovakia —

Slovakia ratified the European Social Charter and Protocol No. 1, which adds new rights, on 22/06/1998. It has accepted 60 of the 72 paragraphs of the Charter and the 4 paragraphs of Protocol No. 1.

Slovakia ratified Protocol No. 2 reforming the control mechanism on 22/06/1998. It has signed but not yet ratified Protocol No. 3 on "collective complaints" and the revised Charter.

In 2000, Slovakia submitted its first report on the application of the Charter. The next report on the hard core provisions is due on 30/06/2003.

Slovakia's record with respect to the application of the Charter is the following as of 1 July 2001:

Cases of non-compliance

Equality (sex)

▶ *Articles 4§3 and §1 of the Add. Prot. – right to equal pay.* The concept of equal pay for work of equal value is not expressly provided for in Slovak law.

Employment

▶ *Article 4§4 – right to notice of termination of employment.* The law does not provide for a reasonable period of notice of termination of employment in every instance.

▶ *Article 8§2 – prohibition of dismissal during maternity leave.* There are several instances where the law allows dismissal during maternity leave.

Social Protection

▶ *Article 16 – rights of the family (family benefit).* The number of families entitled to such benefits is manifestly insufficient.

— Slovenia —

Slovenia ratified the revised European Social Charter on 07/05/1999 and has accepted 95 of the revised Charter's 98 paragraphs.

Slovenia has agreed to be bound by the "collective complaints" procedure. It has not yet made a declaration enabling national NGOs to submit complaints.

The first report on the hard core provisions of the revised Charter was submitted on 13/07/2001.

– Spain –

Spain ratified the European Social Charter on 06/05/1980 and on 24/01/2001 Spain ratified Protocol No. 1 which adds new rights. Spain accepted all 72 paragraphs of the Charter and the 4 paragraphs of Protocol No. 1. On 04/12/1990, it denounced Article 8§4b (prohibition of the employment of women in certain dangerous occupations).

Spain ratified Protocol No. 2 reforming the control mechanism on 24/01/2001. Spain has also signed, but not yet ratified, the revised Charter.

Between 1982 and 2000, Spain submitted 13 reports on the application of the Charter. The next report on the hard core provisions was due on 30/06/2001.

Spain's record with respect to application of the Charter is the following as of 1 July 2001:

Examples of progress achieved or being achieved

General
▶ The Workers' Statute of 10 March 1980 was drafted and adopted with a view to Spain's ratification of the European Social Charter.

Health/Education
▶ More effective preventive role for workers' representatives in the fight against illegal employment, in particular by requiring employers to provide representatives with a "basic copy" of all employment contracts signed, extended or envisaged within the enterprise (Act No. 2 of 7 January 1991). *Article 7§1 - prohibition of the employment of children under the age of 15.*

Employment/Right to organise
▶ Express repeal of the Merchant Navy (Criminal and Disciplinary Offences) Act of 22 December, merchant seamen are now liable to disciplinary sanctions (pecuniary and professional-related) only for the offences listed in Chapters III and IV of Part IV of the 1992 Act (National Ports and Merchant Navy Act No. 27 of 24 November 1992); repeal of Sections 29 and 49 of Act No. 209 of 24 December 1964, whereby flight personnel could be subjected to criminal penalties for disciplinary offences even in cases where neither the safety of the aircraft nor the lives or health of those on board was threatened (Act No. 10 of 23 November 1995 amending the penal code). *Article 1§2 – prohibition of forced labour.*

▶ Abolition of the reciprocity rule applicable to the eligibility of foreign workers to act as shop stewards within firms and abolition of any other discrimination against foreign workers in trade union matters (Trade Union Freedom Act No. 11 of 2 August 1985). *Article 6§1 and 2 – right to bargain collectively: joint consultation and collective bargaining procedures.*

▶ Maintenance of only two categories of wage, based on age: for workers under the age of 18 and workers aged 18 or over (Royal Decree No. 170/1990). *Article 7§5 – right of young people between 15 and 18 to special working conditions (remuneration).*

▶ Improvement in the regulations governing night work for women in industrial jobs: limitation of the duration of night work, definition of night work, higher rate of pay or additional time off (Act No. 11 of 19 May 1994). *Article 8§4 – regulation of night work for women.*

Social Protection

▶ Establishment of a system of non-contributory benefits, including family benefit. *Article 12§3 – right to social security: improvement and safeguard. Article 16 – rights of the family: family benefit.*

▶ Extension of the payment of old-age, invalidity and family benefits to all citizens concerned, in cases where they have insufficient means, including even people who have never contributed or who have not contributed for long enough to qualify for a contributory pension (Act No. 26 of 1990); extension of medical assistance to foreigners resident or lawfully present in Spain (Act No. 13 of 30 December 1996, which entered into force on 1 January 1997). *Article 13§1 – social and medical assistance: individual right to adequate assistance.*

Movement of Persons

▶ *Article 19§8 – right to guarantees in case of expulsion.* More extensive safeguards against the expulsion of foreign nationals (Foreign Nationals Act No. 7 of 1 July 1985 and implementing Royal Decree No. 1119/1986)

Equality

Nationality

▶ *Article 5 – right to organise.* Reinforcement of trade unions' bargaining power by increasing the number of areas that may be covered by collective bargaining (Act No. 7 of 19 July 1990 on collective bargaining and participation in determining the working conditions of public servants).

Sex

▶ Adoption of new legislation designed to eliminate discrimination in employment, including reversal of the burden of proof, requiring defendant employers to demonstrate a reasonable objective justification for the measures in question and their proportionality in cases where it appears from the allegations that there is an element of sex discrimination, including in matters relating to pay (Section 96 of the Labour Procedure Act promulgated by Royal Decree No. 521 of 1990). *Article 1§2 – prohibition of discrimination in employment. Article 4§3 – right to equal pay for work of equal value.*

Cases of non-compliance

Health
▶ *Article 7§9 – right of young people between 15 and 18 to special working conditions: medical supervision.* No legal provision guarantees regular medical supervision for workers under the age of 18 employed in family businesses who do not have the status of paid employees and young self-employed workers not covered by labour law.

Health/Education
▶ *Article 7§1 – prohibition of the employment of children under 15.* No minimum age of admission to employment applies to work within family businesses, or to self-employment.

▶ *Article 7§3 – prohibition of the employment of children under 15.* Spanish law does not guarantee the right of children working in a family business or young self-employed workers to the full benefit of compulsory education.

▶ *Article 7§4 – right of young people between 15 and 18 to special working conditions: working time.* There is no provision in Spanish law which limits the number of working hours of young workers under the age of 16 who are members of their employer's family and who are not registered as employees. In addition, self-employment is not prohibited for children under 18 years, and there are no limits on the number of hours which they may work.

▶ *Article 7§8 – rights of young people (prohibition of night work).* The Spanish government has not demonstrated that the great majority of young people under the age of 18 are prohibited from doing night work.

Education
▶ *Article 7§6 – right of young people between 15 and 18 to special working conditions (time for training).* No specific provision exists, in the form of either legislation or regulations, to ensure that time spent in vocational training during normal working hours with the employer's consent is remunerated as such.

Employment/Right to organise
▶ *Article 2§1 – right to reasonable working time.* The Workers' Statute permits a working week of more than sixty hours.

▶ *Article 4§1 – right to fair remuneration.* The gross minimum wage in 1996 amounted to only 45% of the net average wage, which is far below the 60% threshold. This percentage, moreover, is likely to be even weaker when calculated on the basis of the net minimum wage. A wage that falls so far behind the average in society is manifestly unfair.

▶ *Article 4§2 – right to increased remuneration for overtime.* There is nothing in the law to ensure that workers receive an increased rate of pay or an equivalent rest period, in exchange for overtime.

▶ *Article 4§4 – right to protection in case of dismissal.* Employees on fixed-term contracts of more than one year are entitled to only fifteen days' notice and a worker whose employment is terminated on account of the death, incapacity or retirement of their employer is entitled to only one month's pay, irrespective of length of service

▶ *Article 6§2 – right to collective bargaining: machinery for voluntary negotiations.* The imposition of a wage freeze for public servants in 1997 amounted to intervention in an existing collective agreement which was not justified under Article 31 of the Charter.

▶ *Article 7§5 – right of young people between 15 and 18 to special working conditions: pay.* The minimum wage for adults, which serves as a reference wage, is so low as to be manifestly unfair; the wage of young workers and apprentices is thus not in compliance with this provision of the Charter.

▶ *Article 8§2 – prohibition of dismissal during maternity leave.* Domestic workers do not enjoy the same protection as other workers.

Social Protection

▶ *Article 16 – rights of the family: family benefit.* Equality of treatment is not guaranteed where the payment of family benefit is concerned.

Movement of Persons

▶ *Article 19§8 – right to guarantees in case of expulsion.* The grounds for expulsion go beyond those accepted under Article 19§8. The same applies to self-employed workers.

Equality

▶ *Article 12§4 – right to social security.* Equal treatment is not guaranteed with regard to the payment of family benefit.

▶ *Article 13§1 – individual right to social and medical assistance.* Payment of minimum income benefit is subject to a residence requirement in all parts of the country and to a minimum age requirement, set at twenty-five years, in most of the autonomous communities.

— Sweden —

Sweden ratified the European Social Charter on 17/12/1962 and the revised Charter on 29/05/1998. Sweden has accepted 62 of the Charter's 72 paragraphs and 83 of the revised Charter's 98 paragraphs.

Sweden ratified Protocol No. 3 on the "collective complaints" procedure on 29/05/1998. It has not yet made a declaration enabling national NGOs to submit complaints.

Between 1964 and 2000, Sweden submitted 20 reports on the application of the Charter. The first report on the hard core provisions of the revised Charter was submitted on 03/09/2001.

Sweden's record with respect to application of the Charter is the following as of 1 July 2001:

Examples of progress achieved or being achieved

Health/Education
▶ The Act on the working environment has been extended to cover children under 18 who do not receive any income, including children related to their employer (1990) and those who work in their employer's home (1996). *Article 7§1 – prohibition of child employment under 15.*

Equality

Origin
▶ Adoption of the Act of 7 April 1994 against ethnic discrimination, including in employment. *Article 1§2 – prohibition of discrimination in employment.*

Sex
▶ Adoption of Act No. 433 of 1991 on equal opportunities. *Articles 1§2 and 20 – right of men and women to equal treatment and equal opportunities.*

Employment
▶Abolition of the provision of the legislation governing seafarers which provided that seamen could be bound by coercive measures to remain at their post (Act No. 282 of 18 May 1973 on the Merchant Navy). *Article 1§2- prohibition of forced labour.*

▶Recourse to the closed shop provisions has been made more restrictive (Act of 10 June 1976 on participation in decisions in employment). *Article 5 – right to organise.*

Movement of persons

▶ Abolition of the requirement for employers to pay for language courses for their migrant workers (Repeal in 1986 of Act No. 650 of 1972). *Article 19§5 – right to equal treatment in respect of taxes and dues.*

Cases of non-compliance

Health

▶*Article 7§9 – right of young people between 15 and 18 to special working conditions (medical supervision).* The legislation does not guarantee a regular medical examination for young workers aged under 18 and there are no guarantees in practice.

▶*Article 8§1 – right to maternity leave and benefits.* Swedish legislation does not provide for a period of at least six weeks compulsory postnatal leave.

Education/Health

▶*Article 7§3 – prohibition of child employment under 15.* The compulsory rest period during school holidays for children of compulsory school age is not sufficient to enable them to get the benefit of their schooling.

Movement of persons

▶ *Article 18§3 – right to simplification and liberalisation of formalities related to immigration.* Regulations governing foreign workers' access to the Swedish labour market are too restrictive.

▶*Article 19§6 – right to family reunion.* The Swedish Government has not shown that children of non EU or EEA nationals aged 18 to 21 are entitled in practice to family reunion.

▶*Article 19§8 – right to guarantees in case of expulsion.* A migrant worker expelled on grounds of national security may not appeal to an independent body.

Employment/Right to organise

▶*Article 5 – right to organise* 1. There is no protection in law of the freedom not to join a trade union where a closed shop operates. 2. Closed shop and priority clauses are found in practice.

▶*Article 4§4 – right to notice of dismissal.* Provisions of collective agreements may provide, to an excessive extent, for derogations from the statutory period of notice on dismissal.

▶*Article 8§3 – right to time off for nursing mothers.* Employers are not legally bound to grant employees paid time off for nursing during work hours.

– Turkey –

Turkey ratified the European Social Charter on 24/11/1989. It has accepted 46 of the 72 paragraphs of the Charter.

Turkey has neither signed nor ratified Protocol No. 2 reforming the control mechanism, Protocol No. 3 on "collective complaints" or the revised Charter.

Between 1991 and 2000, Turkey submitted 7 reports on the application of the Charter. The next report on the hard core provisions of the Charter was due on 30/06/2001.

Turkey's record with respect to application of the Charter is the following as of 1 July 2001:

Examples of progress achieved or being achieved

Social protection
▶ Introduction of a system of unemployment benefits (Act reforming certain aspects of the social security system, entered into force on 8 September 1999). *Article 12§1 – right to social security (existence and maintenance of a social security system).*

Equality

Nationality
▶ The monthly poverty benefit (*muhtaçlik ayligi*) paid by the Directorate-General of Trusts and which used to be reserved for Turkish nationals only, has been available to all nationalities since 17 January 1997. *Article 13§1 – right to equal treatment in respect of assistance.*

Sex
▶ A draft law to reform the civil code, ensuring equality between spouses and between parents is currently before parliament. *Article 16 – rights of family (legal protection).*

Education
▶ The duration of compulsory schooling was extended in 1997 and is now 8 years. A draft law aims to extend the protection afforded by Labour Act No. 1475 to include persons employed in agriculture (including the construction of forest roads) in "firms employing three workers which meet the definition

of the Craftsmen and Small Traders Act" and "in any construction work which falls within the scope of a family business" *Article 7 – Rights of children.*

Movement of persons

▶ A draft law of 2 May 1996 extends the duration of the residence permit to five years (instead of the current two years). Other improvements envisaged by the draft law: responsibility for issuing work permits will lie with the Employment Bureau of the Ministry of Labour, rather than with several departments as is currently the case, which will help standardise the procedures for applying for a work permit; a foreign worker who has been working for 2 years or more will be entitled to a five-year residence permit, which will thus take into account the time spent in the country by this worker; a foreign worker who has been employed for 10 years will automatically be granted a permanent work permit; a foreign worker who has been resident in the country for 5 years will be able to apply for a work permit personally, without having to go through an employer. *Article 18§1 – right to liberalisation and simplification of immigration procedures.*

Cases of non-compliance

Health

▶ *Article 7§4 – right of young people between 15 and 18 to special working conditions (working time).* Young people under the age of 16 are covered by Section 61 of the Labour Act which limits the working week to 45 hours which is excessive.

▶ *Article 7§8 – right of young people between 15 and 18 to special working conditions (night work).* Only industrial night work is prohibited in the case of workers under the age of 18.

▶ *Article 7§9 – right of young people between 15 and 18 to special working conditions (medical examination).* 1. The Labour Act does not cover all sectors of economy (the agricultural sector, in particular, is excluded). 2. The frequency of medical examinations for young seafarers is not satisfactory.

▶ *Article 8§1 – right to maternity leave and benefits.* Compulsory six-week post-natal maternity leave is not guaranteed.

▶ *Article 11§1 – right of access to health.* The manifestly inadequate budget for health care and the inadequacy of health care facilities and staff mean that the public, and in particular children, are not guaranteed access to health care nationwide.

▶ *Article 11§3 – right to health protection (regulations and prophylactic measures).* The immunisation rates are inadequate in the case of several diseases.

Employment

▶ *Article 1§2 – prohibition of forced labour.* Under Article 1467 of the Commercial Code (Act No. 6762 of 29 June 1956), the captain of a ship may use force to bring seamen back on board with a view to ensuring the proper running of the vessel and the maintenance of discipline.

Education

▶ *Articles 1§4 and 9 – right to vocational guidance, training and rehabilitation.* The geographical distribution of vocational guidance services is not satisfactory: they are available in only 6 of the 73 Turkish provinces.

▶ *Article 7§3 – prohibition of employment of young people under 15 years.* 1. Children who are still subject to compulsory schooling may be employed in certain sectors of the economy. 2. In 1994-1998, a substantial number of such children were employed and therefore denied the benefit of such education.

Equality

Sex

▶ *Article 4§3 – right to equal pay.* 1. National law does not incorporate the notion of equal remuneration for work of equal value. 2. The statutory limits imposed on compensation for the unlawful dismissal of an employee who has sought to uphold the right to equal pay may deprive such persons of the adequate remedy which this provision of the Charter requires.

Nationality

▶ *Article 12§4 – right to equal treatment in social security matters.* 1. Foreign employees in Turkey do not benefit from equal treatment in social security coverage against long-term risks. 2. Self-employed workers who are nationals of other states fall outside the scope of Act No. 1479 of 2 September 1997 on social insurance for the self-employed. They can neither acquire nor retain rights under Turkish social security legislation. 3. Self-employed refugees and stateless persons are treated as foreign nationals and are excluded from the scope of the Act on the social insurance of self-employed workers. They, too, can neither acquire nor retain rights under Turkish social security legislation.

▶ *Article 13§1 – individual right to social and medical assistance.* The monthly benefit payable under Act No. 2022 of 1 July 1976 to persons over the age of 65 suffering hardship, invalids and disabled persons, is reserved for Turkish nationals only.

▶ *Article 19§4 – right to equal treatment in trade union matters.* Foreign nationals, including nationals of Contracting Parties to the Charter, cannot become founder members of a trade union (Section 5 of the Trade Union Act No. 2821).

Social protection

▶ *Article 13§1 – individual right to social and medical assistance.* The monthly benefit paid under Act No. 2022 of 1 July 1976 to persons over the age of 65 suffering hardship, invalids and disabled persons is not sufficient.

▶ *Article 16 – Rights of family (legal and economic protection).* 1. Certain provisions of the Turkish Civil Code are contrary to the principle of equality between spouses and between parents. 2. Only a small proportion of Turkish families are in receipt of family benefit.

▶ *Article 17 – rights of young people (legal and social protection).* The minimum length of certain prison sentences for young offenders is excessive.

Movement of persons

▶ *Article 18§§2 and 3 – right to simplification and liberalisation of immigration procedures.* 1. Two separate procedures have to be followed when applying for work and residence permits, contrary to the requirement for simplification of procedures. 2. Under existing regulations, work permits are issued to workers who are nationals of Contracting Parties to the Charter for specific jobs with a particular employer.

▶ *Article 19§6 – right to family reunion.* Certain cases in which the health of persons wishing to benefit from family reunification is taken into account in the granting of residence permits exceed what is permissible under this provision of the Charter (cf. Section 8 of the 1950 Passports Act (No. 5682)).

▶ *Article 19§8 – right to guarantees in case of expulsion.* Under Turkish law, the Ministry of the Interior can expel foreigners for reasons solely related to health (Section 19 of Act No. 5683 on the residence and movements of foreigners in Turkey).

— The United Kingdom —

The United Kingdom ratified the European Social Charter on 11/07/1962. The United Kingdom has accepted 60 of the Charter's 72 paragraphs.

The United Kingdom has signed but not yet ratified Protocol No. 2 reforming the control mechanism and the revised Charter. The United Kingdom has not signed or ratified Protocol No. 3 on "collective complaints".

Between 1965 and 2000, the United Kingdom submitted 20 reports on the application of the Charter. The 21st report on the hard core provisions was submitted on 04/09/2001.

The United Kingdom's record with respect to application of the Charter is the following as of 1 July 2001:

Examples of progress achieved or being achieved

Equality

Sex
► Access to a court and recognition of the right of appeal against the certifications provided for under section 79 of the Equal Treatment in Employment Act (Northern Ireland) to justify refusing employment on grounds of safeguarding national security or public order. *Article 1§2 – prohibition of discrimination in employment.*

Nationality
► Eligibility for housing benefit (in the United Kingdom, the Isle of Man, Scotland and Northern Ireland), long tenancies for local authority housing and the right to occupy housing (in Scotland and in Northern Ireland) has been extended to foreign nationals who are citizens of States that are Contracting Parties to the Charter provided that they are habitually resident (orders of 1997, 1998 and 1999 on housing and the homeless). *Article 19§4 – right to equal treatment in housing.*

Employment
► The Government is committed to repealing section 59 of the Merchant Shipping Act 1995 which permits sanctions against seamen. *Article 1§2 – prohibition of forced labour.*

Right to organise

▶ Dismissing an employee under a *closed shop* agreement is considered unfair and affords a right of action (Employment Act 1982). Any dismissal on the ground of membership or non-membership of a trade union is automatically unfair (Employment Act 1988). Any discrimination on grounds of membership or non-membership of a trade union on recruitment is unlawful (Employment Act 1990)

▶ The confidentiality of trade union membership is protected (Employment Relations Act 1999). *Article 5 – right to organise.*

▶ The ways in which collective action can be prevented have been relaxed (Employment Relations Act 1999). *Article 6§4 – right to collective bargaining (strikes and lock-outs).*

Social Protection

▶ *Statutory Maternity Pay* (SMP) has been increased substantially (provisions on maternity protection as amended) *Article 8§1 – right to maternity benefits.*

▶ Corporal punishment has been abolished in both State schools and grant-maintained schools in the United Kingdom (Education Act 1986 (No. 2)). *Article 17 – right of young persons (legal and social protection).*

Movement of persons

▶ An appeal may be brought before the Immigration Appeals Tribunal against deportation orders made by the Home Secretary on grounds of national security or for political reasons (1997 Act governing the Special Immigration Appeals Commission). *Article 19§8 – right to guarantees in case of expulsion.*

Cases of non-compliance

Health

▶ *Article 8§1 – right to maternity leave.* Six weeks' compulsory postnatal maternity leave is not guaranteed.

Equality (nationality)

Discrimination against non EU or EEA nationals in the following matters:

▶ Grant of housing benefit, access to long-term tenancies in social housing and authorisation to occupy housing (requirement of habitual residence). *Article 19§4 – right to equal treatment with respect to housing.*

▶ Payment of family allowance (subject to a children's residence requirement). *Article 16 – right to equal treatment with respect to family benefits.*

Education
▶ *Article 7§3 – prohibition of child employment under 15.* The compulsory rest period during school holiday to which children of compulsory school age are entitled is not sufficient to ensure that they fully benefit from that education.

Social Protection
▶ *Article 8§1 – right to maternity leave.* The amount of Statutory Maternity Pay (SMP) paid after six weeks is insufficient

▶ *Article 13§1 – individual right to adequate assistance.* The grant of social assistance is subject to a requirement of habitual residence, meaning not only an intention to reside in the United Kingdom but also the existence of an "appreciable period of residence" in the territory.

Employment
▶ *Article 1§2 – prohibition of forced labour.* Sanctions may be imposed on striking seamen (Section 59 of the Merchant Shipping Act 1995)

▶ *Articles 4§1 (adults) and 7§5 (young persons) – right to fair remuneration.* 1. The net wage of an employee receiving GBP 187.8 per week (half the average national wage in 1997) is equivalent to only 53% of the average net national wage. 2. A substantial number of employees receive a markedly lower wage.

▶ *Article 4§2 – right to increased remuneration for overtime.* The Government has not shown that in practice all employees enjoy guaranteed increased remuneration for overtime.

▶ *Article 4§4 – right to notice of dismissal.* The statutory periods of notice for workers of up to three years standing are not reasonable.

Right to organise
▶ *Article 5 – right to organise.* 1. Excessive restriction of trade unions' right to make free use of their property and possessions (Section 15 of the Trade Union and Labour Relations (C) Act 1992); 2. Excessive restriction of trade unions' right to refuse membership or to expel a member (Sections 64-67 of the Trade Union and Labour Relations (C) Act 1992); 3. Possibility for employers to take certain measures in order to persuade employees to relinquish trade union representation and collective bargaining; 4. Excessive restriction of trade unions' right with regard to disciplinary action against their members (Sections 174-177 of the Trade Union and Labour Relations (C) Act 1992).

▶ *Article 6§4 – right to collective bargaining (strikes and lock-outs).* 1. The law is unduly restrictive of possibilities for collective action (Sections 226-228 of the Trade Union and Labour Relations (C) Act 1992); 2. Possibility for an employer to dismiss all employees taking part in collective action (Section 237 of the Trade Union and Labour Relations (C) Act 1992).

Movement of persons

▶ *Article 18§3 – right to simplification and liberalisation of formalities related to immigration.* The conditions imposed on the employment of foreigners who are non EU nationals are excessively restrictive.

▶ *Article 13§4 – right to emergency assistance until repatriation.* There is no adequate emergency assistance provided for by the public authorities (accommodation, food, clothing etc.) for foreigners who are lawfully in the United Kingdom without also being resident there.

General Overview of National Situations

General Overview of National Situations

Legend: + In conformity   – Not in conformity   0 Deferred Decision   Grey Squares are non-accepted provisions

Article	AU	BE	CY	DK	FI	FR	GE	GR	IC	IR	IT	LU	MA	NE	NO	POL	POR	SL	SP	SW	TU	UK
Article 1.2 FL	+	–	–	–	+	–	+	–	+	+	–	+	+	–	+	0	–	+	+	+	–	–
Article 1.2 ND	+	+	+	+	+	+	+	–	+	+	0	+	+	+	+	0	+	0	+	+	0	–
Article 1.3	+	0	+	+	0	+	+	–	+	0	0	+	0	+	+	+	+	0	0	+	0	+
Article 1.4	–		+	0	0	+	+	0	0	0	0	0	0	+	+		0	0	+	+		+
Article 2.1		–	0		–	+	+	0	–	–	0	0	0	–	–	0	+	0	–			
Article 2.2	+	–	+	+		+	+	0		+	+	+	+	+	+		–	0	+	+		+
Article 2.3	+	+	+	+	+	+	+	+	+	+	0	+	+	+	+	+	+	0	+	+		0
Article 2.4	0	–			+	+	+	+			–	–	–	–	+	0	0	+	0			0
Article 2.5	+	+	+	+	0	+	+	+	+	0	+	+		0	+	+	+	0	0	+		0
Article 3.1	+	+	+	+		0	+	+	0	+	–	0	+	–	+	0	+	+	0	+		+
Article 3.2	0	0	+	+		+	+	+	0	0	0	0	0	0	+	+	–	+	0	+	0	+
Article 3.3	+	+	+	+	+	+	0	0	+	0	+	+	0	0	+	0	+	+	+	+	0	+
Article 4.1	0	0	0	0		0	0	0	0	+	0	0	+	–	0		0	0	+	0		–
Article 4.2	+	–	+	+	0	+	+	0	+	–	0	0	0	+	+	–	0	0	–			–
Article 4.3	+	–			0	+	+	–	0		0	–	0	0	0	0	–	–	0	+	–	–
Article 4.4	+	–	+	+		+	+	–	0	0	–	0	0	0	+	–	0	–	–	–		–
Article 4.5	+	+	+	0	0	+	+	+	+	0	+	0	0	+	+	0	+	0	+		0	0
Article 5	–	0	+	–	–	0	+		–	–	+	–	–	+	+	0	–	0	–	–	0	–
Article 6.1	+	+	+	+	+	+	+		+	0	+	+	0	+	+	+	+	0	+	+		0
Article 6.2	+	+	–	–	+	0	+		+	–	+	+	–	+	+	+	+	0	+	+		–
Article 6.3	0	+	+	0	+	+	+		+	+	+	+	–	+	–	+	+	0	+	+		0
Article 6.4		0	0	–	0	–	–	–	–	–	0		0	0	–		0	0	0	+		–

Article	AU	BE	CY	DK	FI	FR	GE	GR	IC	IR	IT	LU	MA	NE	NO	POL	POR	SL	SP	SW	TU	UK
Article 7.1	+	+	+		+	-	+	0			-	+	+	+	+		-	0	-	+		
Article 7.2	+	+			+	+	+			+	+	+	+	+	+	+	+	0	+	+		+
Article 7.3	0	+	+		0	-	-	0		-	-	+	-	-	-		+	0	-	+	-	-
Article 7.4	+	+			0	+	+	+		0	-	-	+	0		+	+	0	-	+	-	
Article 7.5	0	-			0	0	0	0		-	0	-	+	-	0		0	0	-		0	-
Article 7.6		+				+	+	+		+	+	+	+	-	+	+	+	0	-	+	0	+
Article 7.7	+	0	+		+	+	+	+			+	+	+	+	+	+	+	+	+	+		
Article 7.8	+	0	-		+	+	+	0			+	+	0	+	+	+	-	+	-	+	-	+
Article 7.9	+	+	+			+	+	+		+	+	+	+	0		+	+	0	+	-	-	+
Article 7.10	+				+	+	+	+			+	+	+	+	+	+	+	+	+	+		-
Article 8.1 i	+	+	0	-		+	+	0	+	0	+	+	-	-		+	-	-	0	0		-
Article 8.1 ii	+	+	0	0	-	-	+		+	0	0	+	-	-			+	0	-			
Article 8.2	+	-	-			-		+	+	0	0	0		0	+	0	+	-	+	-		
Article 8.3	+	-				-	+	0	+	-	-	+	+	+		+	+	0	0			
Article 8.4 a	0	0	0		0	0		+	+	0	+		0	0		0	0	0	+	+	-	
Article 8.4 b	0	+				0	+	+			-	+	+	+		+	+	+	0	+	0	
Article 9	+	0	+	+	0	+	+	+	+	+	0	+	+	0	+	0	0	0	+	+	+	+
Article 10.1	0	0		+	+	+	+	+	+	0	0	0	0	+	+	0	0	0	+	+	0	+
Article 10.2	-	0		+	0	+	+	+	+	0	+	0	0	+	+	0	0	0	+	+	+	+
Article 10.3	+	0		0	0	+	0	+	+	0	0	0	0	+	+	0	0	0	+	+	0	+
Article 10.4	0	-		0	-	+	+	0		0	0	0	+	+	+		0	0	+	+	0	+
Article 11.1	+	0	0	+	+	+	+	+	+	0	0	0	0	+	+	0	0	0	+	+	-	0
Article 11.2	0	0		0	+	+		-		+	0	0	0	+	+	0	+	0	0	+	0	+
Article 11.3	+	-	0	+	+	+	+	+	+		+	0	0	+	+	0	+	0	+	+	-	0
Article 12.1	+	+	+	+	+	+	+	+	+	+	+	+	+	+	+	+	+	0	+	+	+	0
Article 12.2	+	+	+	+	+	+	+	+		+	+	+		+	+	0	+	0	+	+	0	
Article 12.3	+	+	+	+	+	+		+	+		0	+	+	-	-	0	+	0	-	+	0	
Article 12.4	-	-	-		-	-		-	-	-	-		+	+	-	0	-	0			-	

Article	AU	BE	CY	DK	FI	FR	GE	GR	IC	IR	IT	LU	MA	NE	NO	POL	POR	SL	SP	SW	TU	UK
Article 13.1	+	0			+	+	+	+	+	+	+	+	+	+	+		+	0	+	+	-	-
Article 13.2	+	+		+	+	+	+	+	+	+	+	+	+	+	+	+	+	+	+	+	+	+
Article 13.3	+	+		0	+	+		+	0	+	0	+	+	+	+	0	+	0	+	+	-	+
Article 13.4	+	+	+	+	+	+	0	+	0	+	+	0	+	0	+	0	+		0	+	+	-
Article 14.1	+	+	+		+	+	+	+	+	+	+	+	+	+	+	0	+	0	0	+	0	+
Article 14.2	+	+		+	+	+	+	+	+	+	+	+	+	+	+		+	+	0	+	+	+
Article 15.1	+	-		+	0	+	+	0	+	0	0	0	+	+	+	0	0		0			+
Article 15.2	+	-		+	-	+	+	0	-	0	-	0	+	+	0	0	0		0	+		+
Article 16		-		-	-	-	+	-	-	-	-	-	+	-	-	-	+	0	-	+	-	-
Article 17		0		0	+	-	+	+	-	0	0	0		0	+	0	+	0	0	-	+	0
Article 18.1	0	0		0	0	0	+	-	0	0	0	+		0	+		+	0	+	+	+	+
Article 18.2	0	0		0	0	+	+	+	0	0	0	+		0	+	+		0	0	+	+	-
Article 18.3	+	0		-	0	0	0	-	0	0	0	0		+	0	+	+	0	+	+	-	0
Article 18.4	+	0		+	+	+	+	+	+	+	+	+	+	+	+	-	+	+	+	+	0	+
Article 19.1	+	+			+	+	+	+	+	+	+	+		+	+	+	+		+	+	+	+
Article 19.2	+	+	+	+	0	+	+	+	+	+	+	0		+	+	+	+		0	+	+	+
Article 19.3	+	+	0	0	+	+	-	+	+	+	+	+		+	0	-	+	+	+	+	-	-
Article 19.4	+	+	+	+	+	+	+	+	+	+	+	+	+	+	+	+	+	0	+	+	-	-
Article 19.5	+	+	+	+	+	+	+	+	+	+	+	-		+	+	+	+	0	0	+	-	+
Article 19.6	-	-		0	0	+	-	+	-	+	+	0		+	+	0	0	+	+	-	-	0
Article 19.7		+	+	-	-	+	+	+	+	+	+	+		+	+	0	+	+	+	+	+	+
Article 19.8	+	+	0	0	0	+	-	+	+	+	+	-	+	+	+	-	+	0	0		-	+
Article 19.9	+	+	+	+	+	+	+	+	+	+	+	-	+	+	+	0	+	0	+	+	-	+
Article 19.10		-		+	0	+	-	+	-	-	-	-		-	+	-	+	0	-	+	-	-
AP Article 1					0						0			+	+			-	0	0		
AP Article 2					+						0			+	0			+	+	0		
AP Article 3					+						0			+	0			0	0	+		
AP Article 4					0						0				+			0	0	+		

Sales agents for publications of the Council of Europe
Agents de vente des publications du Conseil de l'Europe

AUSTRALIA/AUSTRALIE
Hunter Publications, 58A, Gipps Street
AUS-3066 COLLINGWOOD, Victoria
Tel.: (61) 3 9417 5361
Fax: (61) 3 9419 7154
E-mail: Sales@hunter-pubs.com.au
http://www.hunter-pubs.com.au

AUSTRIA/AUTRICHE
Gerold und Co., Weihburggasse 26
A-1011 WIEN
Tel.: (43) 1 533 5014
Fax: (43) 1 533 5014 18
E-mail: buch@gerold.telecom.at
http://www.gerold.at

BELGIUM/BELGIQUE
La Librairie européenne SA
50, avenue A. Jonnart
B-1200 BRUXELLES 20
Tel.: (32) 2 734 0281
Fax: (32) 2 735 0860
E-mail: info@libeurop.be
http://www.libeurop.be

Jean de Lannoy
202, avenue du Roi
B-1190 BRUXELLES
Tel.: (32) 2 538 4308
Fax: (32) 2 538 0841
E-mail: jean.de.lannoy@euronet.be
http://www.jean-de-lannoy.be

CANADA
Renouf Publishing Company Limited
5369 Chemin Canotek Road
CDN-OTTAWA, Ontario, K1J 9J3
Tel.: (1) 613 745 2665
Fax: (1) 613 745 7660
E-mail: order.dept@renoufbooks.com
http://www.renoufbooks.com

CZECH REPUBLIC/RÉPUBLIQUE TCHÈQUE
Suweco Cz Dovoz Tisku Praha
Ceskomoravska 21
CZ-18021 PRAHA 9
Tel.: (420) 2 660 35 364
Fax: (420) 2 683 30 42
E-mail: import@suweco.cz

DENMARK/DANEMARK
Swets Blackwell A/S
Jagtvej 169 B, 2 Sal
DK-2100 KOBENHAVN O
Tel.: (45) 39 15 79 15
Fax: (45) 39 15 79 10
E-mail: info@dk.swetsblackwell.com

FINLAND/FINLANDE
Akateeminen Kirjakauppa
Keskuskatu 1, PO Box 218
FIN-00381 HELSINKI
Tel.: (358) 9 121 41
Fax: (358) 9 121 4450
E-mail: akatilaus@stockmann.fi
http://www.akatilaus.akateeminen.com

FRANCE
La Documentation française
(Diffusion / Vente France entière)
124 rue H. Barbusse
93308 Aubervilliers Cedex
Tel.: (33) 01 40 15 70 00
Fax: (33) 01 40 15 68 00
E-mail: vel@ladocfrancaise.gouv.fr
http://www.ladocfrancaise.gouv.fr

Librairie Kléber (Vente Strasbourg)
Palais de l'Europe
F-67075 Strasbourg Cedex
Fax: (33) 03 88 52 91 21
E-mail: librairie.kleber@coe.int

GERMANY/ALLEMAGNE
UNO Verlag
Am Hofgarten 10
D-53113 BONN
Tel.: (49) 2 28 94 90 20
Fax: (49) 2 28 94 90 222
E-mail: bestellung@uno-verlag.de
http://www.uno-verlag.de

GREECE/GRÈCE
Librairie Kauffmann
Mavrokordatou 9
GR-ATHINAI 106 78
Tel.: (30) 1 38 29 283
Fax: (30) 1 38 33 967
E-mail: ord@otenet.gr

HUNGARY/HONGRIE
Euro Info Service
Hungexpo Europa Kozpont ter 1
H-1101 BUDAPEST
Tel.: (361) 264 8270
Fax: (361) 264 8271
E-mail: euroinfo@euroinfo.hu
http://www.euroinfo.hu

ITALY/ITALIE
Libreria Commissionaria Sansoni
Via Duca di Calabria 1/1, CP 552
I-50125 FIRENZE
Tel.: (39) 556 4831
Fax: (39) 556 41257
E-mail: licosa@licosa.com
http://www.licosa.com

NETHERLANDS/PAYS-BAS
De Lindeboom Internationale
Publikaties
PO Box 202, MA de Ruyterstraat 20 A
NL-7480 AE HAAKSBERGEN
Tel.: (31) 53 574 0004
Fax: (31) 53 572 9296
E-mail: lindeboo@worldonline.nl
http://home-1-worldonline.nl/~lindeboo/

NORWAY/NORVÈGE
Akademika, A/S Universitetsbokhandel
PO Box 84, Blindern
N-0314 OSLO
Tel.: (47) 22 85 30 30
Fax: (47) 23 12 24 20

POLAND/POLOGNE
Glowna Ksiegarnia Naukowa
im. B. Prusa
Krakowskie Przedmiescie 7
PL-00-068 WARSZAWA
Tel.: (48) 29 22 66
Fax: (48) 22 26 64 49
E-mail: inter@internews.com.pl
http://www.internews.com.pl

PORTUGAL
Livraria Portugal
Rua do Carmo, 70
P-1200 LISBOA
Tel.: (351) 13 47 49 82
Fax: (351) 13 47 02 64
E-mail: liv.portugal@mail.telepac.pt

SPAIN/ESPAGNE
Mundi-Prensa Libros SA
Castelló 37
E-28001 MADRID
Tel.: (34) 914 36 37 00
Fax: (34) 915 75 39 98
E-mail: libreria@mundiprensa.es
http://www.mundiprensa.com

SWITZERLAND/SUISSE
Bersy
Route de Monteiller
CH-1965 SAVIESE
Tél.: (41) 27 395 53 33
Fax: (41) 27 395 53 34
E-mail: jprausis@netplus.ch

Adeco – Van Diermen
Chemin du Lacuez 41
CH-1807 BLONAY
Tel.: (41) 21 943 26 73
Fax: (41) 21 943 36 06
E-mail: mvandier@worldcom.ch

UNITED KINGDOM/ROYAUME-UNI
TSO (formerly HMSO)
51 Nine Elms Lane
GB-LONDON SW8 5DR
Tel.: (44) 207 873 8372
Fax: (44) 207 873 8200
E-mail:
customer.services@theso.co.uk
http://www.the-stationery-office.co.uk
http://www.itsofficial.net

UNITED STATES and CANADA/ ÉTATS-UNIS et CANADA
Manhattan Publishing Company
468 Albany Post Road, PO Box 850
CROTON-ON-HUDSON,
NY 10520, USA
Tel.: (1) 914 271 5194
Fax: (1) 914 271 5856
E-mail:
Info@manhattanpublishing.com
http://www.manhattanpublishing.com

HOW

LEADERS

CREATE

CHAOS

Cover design by: Joe De Leon
Cover Photo by: Andrew van Tilborgh

ISBN: 978-1-959095-35-4   1 2 3 4 5 6 7 8 9 10

Printed in the United States of America

HOW

LEADERS

CREATE

CHAOS

AND WHY THEY SHOULD!

SAM CHAND

AVAIL

KEEP ROARING!

CONTENTS

CHAPTER 1

STABILITY ISN'T YOUR FRIEND!

A minister, without boldness, is like a smooth file, a knife without an edge, a sentinel that is afraid to let off his gun.

—William Gurnall

L ions fascinate me. I've had the opportunity to see them in the wild in Africa, and if a nature program about the African savannah is on television, I can sit for hours watching "the king of beasts." There is no doubt who is in charge—every animal is looking, listening, and smelling the air to see if a lion is nearby. Lions aren't the biggest animals on the savannah, but they have the biggest hearts. Wherever they step, things change. To me, lions are the best metaphor for exemplary leadership—men and women who create chaos wherever they go, making a difference with their presence and shaking up the status quo. When they take a step, everyone shifts to make room. When they have a vision of a better future, nothing will stop them. (Okay, okay, I know leaders don't eat their people, but please stay with me a little bit longer.)

LIONS are the best metaphor for exemplary leadership—men and women who create chaos wherever they go, making a difference with their presence and shaking up the status quo.

I've seen leaders who launched their careers as bold, roaring lions but became tame, overgrown house cats. Their vision, zeal, and passion subsided—often gradually, but sometimes in an accelerated way in critical moments of failure or unexpected opposition (or both). Sooner or later, they didn't *think* like lions, they didn't *feel* like lions, and they didn't *act* like lions. Their roar had become a meow. They began as world-changers, but they became organizational tweakers. Certainly, they didn't look in the mirror one morning and decide to be tame, to avoid making anyone uncomfortable, or to redefine their vision to a bite-sized morsel ... but it happened. If they have enough self-awareness, they wonder, *What in the world happened to me?*

All leaders face "chaotic moments," times that make or break their confidence and their reputations. But it's not just "them." When I look back at my history, I see particular times when these moments suddenly surfaced in my life.

In July of 1980, my wife, Brenda, and I moved to Hartford, Michigan, where I accepted the call to be the Pastor of a small, rural church. Actually, the church was more than three miles from the little town. The closest blinking light was more than two miles from the church. The nearest McDonald's was eighteen miles away. When I stepped through the door of the church for the first time, I was a lion. I saw myself as a change agent, someone who would lead men and women to do magnificent things for God and transform their community. My daydreams painted vivid pictures of remarkable growth in our church and rich discipleship among our people. We would be known as a congregation that eagerly fulfilled the Great Commandment and the Great Commission, and I had a lot of ideas about what we could do.

Before my first Board meeting, just days after we moved into the parsonage, which shared a wall with the church, I looked at church listings in the local yellow pages. (Remember those? If you're under forty, probably not.) I saw that it was possible for us to put our church's name and information in a box, so it would stand out from the rest. When I called the phone company, I was told the additional charge would be only $5 a month. In the Board meeting that first week, I made the recommendation to spend this very modest sum, but the men in the room flatly turned me down. In that moment, a thousand thoughts sped through my mind. *If they wouldn't respect my leadership enough to spend $5 a month to give our church a little more recognition, what did it mean for my future there?*

It was obvious that they didn't see me as an inspiring, effective leader; I was just the hired "main event" on Sunday mornings, Sunday nights, Sunday school, and Wednesday nights—that's four different messages every week. But that's not all. A couple in the church could have stepped out of a movie about the feud between the Hatfields and McCoys. They were fierce and always ready for a fight. They'd run off previous Pastors, and they were proud of their place of power in the church . . . and now they had their sights set on me. I had walked into a room full of explosives, and I was carrying a lit match!

The Board's refusal to spend a few dollars and the couple's antagonism created a chaotic moment that knocked me back and threatened to destroy my confidence . . . but thankfully, I saw the choice very clearly. I was determined to use that moment as a turning point for my thinking, my communication, and my role as the Pastor of the church. It took me three years to change the culture of our congregation, and it was a struggle every step of the way ... but it was absolutely necessary. Slowly, the Board and the people of the church began to see me as their leader, not just the preacher.

I often tell young Pastors that they can have all the high hopes in the world, but when they walk into a new situation, the people there have their own expectations—and almost always, very clear and strong expectations that aren't aligned with the new kid on the block.

> I OFTEN tell young Pastors that they can have all the high hopes in the world, but when they walk into a new situation, the people there have their own expectations ... that aren't aligned with the new kid on the block.

TAKING ADVANTAGE OF THE UNEXPECTED

During the time of cultural transformation in our little church, God used another crucial, chaotic moment to change how people viewed me and the process of transformation I was trying to implement. Bill and Charlene had been members of the church for decades, long before I arrived. Bill was a salt-of-the-earth kind of guy, a hardworking, no-nonsense factory worker who was dedicated to his family and the Lord. Before I arrived, Charlene had been diagnosed with brain cancer, and she struggled with it for a long time. In fact, it took months and many different doctors to finally provide an accurate diagnosis of her medical problem. I visited her many times when she was in the hospital. One evening, their son called to tell me, "Pastor, Mom has been rushed to the Mayo Clinic. She's having brain surgery tomorrow morning. I think this is serious."

The Mayo Clinic is in Rochester, Minnesota, 460 miles from Hartford. In my description of my first calling, I may have neglected to include the fact that my salary at the church was very, very meager. I didn't even have enough money to pay for gas to travel to Rochester, so I went to the home of one of the deacons to ask if I could borrow $200 for the trip. He motioned for me to follow him into his bedroom. We slid the bed to one side, and he removed some planks from the floor, exposing a small safe sitting on the dirt under the house. He took out $200 and gave it to me.

Immediately, I filled up the tank in my little Mazda GLC hatchback and headed west down the highway. I drove all night and arrived at the Mayo Clinic at about five o'clock the next morning. I asked the receptionist for directions to the waiting area near the operating room. When I got to the floor where Charlene was waiting to go to surgery, Bill saw me walking toward him. He ran to me and literally leaped into my arms. He hugged me and wept for a long time. There were no other family members there—just Bill and me. He showed me into Charlene's room, and I prayed for her. When they wheeled her into surgery, Bill and I began our vigil.

Charlene came through the surgery, and later that evening, Bill and I found a little bed and breakfast across the street from the hospital. The price for a room was $15 a night. Neither of us had much money, so we only got one room ... with one bed. Something unspoken but incredibly powerful happened when the two of us slept in the same bed across the street from his beloved wife. I stayed with Bill and Charlene for four days. By this time, it was Saturday, and I had to get back for church the next morning. Before I got in the car, Bill gave me a long hug and wept again with gratitude.

On the drive back to Hartford, I suddenly realized I'd taken a risk by leaving town to be with Bill and Charlene. Would people be upset that I wasn't in town during the week? Would the Board be angry that I spent so much time away from the church? What kind of chaos had I left behind when I drove to Rochester several days earlier?

The next morning in church, I could tell immediately that something was different. Word had gotten out that I had gone to the Mayo Clinic to be with Bill and Charlene, and in that chaotic moment, they now saw me as their Pastor, not just the hired gun: the preacher. When I walked in, people spontaneously came over to hug me, and many people gave me money to pay for the trip—more than enough to repay the $200 loan. The hugs and the money were ways they were saying, "Thank you, Pastor Sam, for caring so much about people we love."

On that day, the bitter couple who had wielded so much power to get rid of Pastors were totally outnumbered by those who now saw me as their Pastor, their shepherd, and their leader. God had caused my response during a moment of chaos to change the culture of our church. No one expected me to borrow money and drive all night to be with Bill and Charlene early in the morning before her surgery. No one expected me to stay there for four days to comfort and support them. And no one expected Bill and me to become bunkmates and bond to become close friends.

INTENTIONAL CHAOS

I've had other chaotic moments that proved to be a launch pad of growth, but each time, things looked very bleak at first. I became the president of Beulah Heights Bible College in southeast Atlanta in July of 1989. The school was dying. It had only eighty-seven students and was without accreditation. I hoped for a quick turnaround, but within a semester, our student enrollment dropped even further. I was very discouraged. During the darkest time for the school and for my confidence, I was asked to preach in south Georgia. On my way back that Sunday night (in the same little Mazda), I poured my heart out to the Lord. I cried tears of heartache and disappointment. I had no idea how to lead this dying organization. I prayed, "Lord, this doesn't make any sense. I thought You told me to go there, but it's not working out at all!"

In that chaotic moment, God gave me a voice and a picture. I sensed Him say, *Take care of My bride, and I'll take care of you.* That wasn't too hard to figure out. The church is the bride of Christ, and He wanted me to devote myself to the people He loves. The picture took a little more time to decipher: It was a white pond with white fish next to a black pond with black fish. There were a lot of fishermen at the white pond but very few at the black one.

The next morning as soon as I got to my office, I began responding to the voice of God. I picked up my copy of the yellow pages (there seems to be a theme here!) and found the list of churches in our area. I began calling each one and asked to speak to the Pastor. I told them, "My name is Sam Chand. I'm the president of Beulah Heights Bible College, and we want to serve you. We would be happy to schedule any kind of training your people might want or need. How can our professors and I serve you?"

Almost without exception, the Pastors responded, "How much does it cost?"

I answered, "Absolutely nothing. We simply want to serve you and your people." This statement usually produced a moment of stunned silence, so I filled in the empty space by explaining, "If you want to schedule two hours on a Saturday morning, we'll send one or two of our professors, or I might come to do the training. The topic is entirely up to you. We can speak on evangelism, discipleship, leading groups, Bible study methods, church polity, lay counseling, and many other subjects. We can train those who serve in childcare, youth workers, or those who teach your classes. All you need to do is get them into the room, and we'll take it from there. We'll do all the preparations."

This effort was the product of an epiphany. At the time, Bible colleges were taking on a life of their own, and many church leaders wondered if these schools expected to be served instead of serving the churches. I realized that God had instituted the church—not Bible colleges—as the body of Christ. The church is central to God's plan and strategy; the schools exist only to help the church thrive, and if the church thrives, Bible colleges will thrive.

GOD instituted the church—not Bible colleges—as the body of Christ. The church is central to God's plan and strategy.

I'm not sure if it's surprising or not, but many of the Pastors I called took us up on our offer. We held training sessions in dozens of churches in our area, and strong relationships developed. Their people got the very best of what we had to offer, and we had the pleasure of sharing our talents with people we would never have met in any other way.

Many of these Pastors and their churches were Black, the predominant ethnicity in southeast Atlanta. It took me a while to realize that this was the answer to the confusing picture God had given me on the drive back from south Georgia. He had put our school in a black pond with plenty of black fish, and we joined the few fishermen on the bank.

When God communicated His heart to me on the drive home from the preaching, Beulah Heights wasn't ready for a turnaround and rapid growth. Our systems were outdated, our administrators didn't have the necessary skills, and our ability to recruit and serve students wasn't what it needed to be. Our efforts in the community, though, sharpened us. And soon, Pastors began calling me to ask, "Are there any openings at your college for students from our church?"

"Yes, Pastor," I always replied. "We'd be happy to have them."

Students at other Bible colleges are usually fresh out of high school, but the people we were training in churches on Saturdays were adults. As some of them enrolled in our school, the demographics of our school suddenly and radically changed. Most of the new students were in their forties, and we had to make significant adjustments to serve them well. For instance, they already had full-time jobs, so they didn't have time to wait in long lines, and they didn't want to discuss grants and financial aid in public settings. The biggest transition for us, though, wasn't the age of our new students. Beulah Heights had been a predominately White school, but now we had a large influx of Black students. We also weren't ready for a much wider range of denominational backgrounds. Our history had been as a White, Pentecostal school, but now we had applicants from Baptist, Methodist, Episcopal, African Methodist Episcopal, and dozens of other faith traditions.

Another change was our school governance. Beulah Heights had been founded by a woman, but when I arrived, the administration and the Board were all White men, as were most of our professors. I began recruiting Black and female administrators, professors, and Board members, and before long, our Board chairman was a distinguished Black man, Dr. Oliver Haney.

In all of these transitions, I was creating chaos every minute of every day! I had people on our administrative team who weren't comfortable with adult students because the adults weren't as malleable as eighteen-year-olds. Our administrators weren't comfortable with so many Black students, and they weren't too sure about the faith of those who came from outside the Pentecostal traditions. We had some intense conversations about what these changes meant for those of us in leadership and for the school itself. For instance, when we accepted students who weren't from Pentecostal backgrounds, we retained our requirement for professors to agree with our statement of faith and practice, but we asked our students to sign a statement that they "understand and respect" those who practice their faith in different ways.

Thankfully, God worked in and through all the changes. When I left Beulah Heights years later, we had dual accreditation with more than eight hundred students from over forty countries and about fifty different denominations. Those numbers sound good, but this kind of growth created chaos everywhere we looked. For instance, we didn't have enough parking for our staff and students, we didn't have enough classrooms, and we didn't have enough toilets for all the people who needed them between classes. Our adult students had a very different perspective on their time, their money, and their education. Our campus policy was that if a professor was more than ten minutes late, the class was dismissed with no penalty for the students. The young students were thrilled when this happened, but the adult students believed their sacrifice of time and money had been wasted, at least for that class period, and many of them wanted a refund or a make-up class. These weren't minor problems, but they were a cheap price to pay for the remarkable growth of our school.

MANAGING OR LEADING?

Many people confuse managers and leaders. Both run meetings, both have important responsibilities, and both are expected to get the job done, but there's a very important difference: managers try to relieve chaos by smoothing out the process, but leaders create healthy chaos to meet needs and move the organization forward. I have a painting in my office about the fundamental nature of leadership. It shows a giraffe looking over the African savannah, and the banner along the bottom reads, "Leadership: Seeing further down the road than those around me can." And seeing further down the road inevitably leads to a bigger vision and faith-stretching plans ... which always create chaos throughout the organization.

THERE'S a very important difference between
managers and leaders: managers try to relieve
chaos by smoothing out the process, but
leaders create healthy chaos to meet needs
and move the organization forward.

Actually, leaders often sense needs before they visualize the future. They feel an urgency to meet the needs even though the people around them don't feel it at all. Leaders answer the only two essential organizational questions: What? and Why? All the other questions—Who? When? Where? How? and How much?—are management questions. Leaders must remain focused on the *strategic* questions. Managers fill in the *tactical* details. The apostle Paul never took his eyes off his God-given calling. In his second letter to the Christians in Corinth, he described the difficulties he faced day after day in all the cities he visited. He explained the enormous tension between his frailty and God's power: "But we have this treasure in jars of clay to show that this all-surpassing power is from God and not from us" (4:7). And just a few verses later, he concluded that spiritual perception was what gave him the courage to keep moving forward:

Therefore we do not lose heart. Though outwardly we are wasting away, yet inwardly we are being renewed day by day. For our light and momentary troubles are achieving for us an eternal glory that far outweighs them all. So we fix our eyes not on what is seen, but on what is unseen, since

what is seen is temporary, but what is unseen is eternal.
—*2 Corinthians 4:16-18*

In the church, however, many people can get confused when they sense healthy and necessary chaos. They wonder, *Didn't Jesus promise us peace? That doesn't sound chaotic to me!* On the night He was betrayed, Jesus spent time with His disciples. He explained more about His purpose, His Kingdom, and the Holy Spirit's role in their lives, and He told them that He grants peace in the midst of chaos—not by eliminating it: "Peace I leave with you; my peace I give you. I do not give to you as the world gives. Do not let your hearts be troubled and do not be afraid" (John 14:27). In other words, reaching the world, building the church, and "doing greater things" always produces internal and external disruption, which I'm calling *chaos.*

A bold vision inevitably creates chaos. If you think your people are "a bit slow on the uptake" when you communicate your vision, you're in good company. Immediately after Jesus fed the four thousand, He and His disciples got in a boat to cross to the other side of the Sea of Galilee. On the way, the men looked into their lunch sack and realized they had only one loaf of bread. They were worried about going hungry! Jesus asked them,

> *"Why are you talking about having no bread? Do you still not see or understand? Are your hearts hardened? Do you have eyes but fail to see, and ears but fail to hear? And don't you remember? When I broke the five loaves for the five thousand, how many basketfuls of pieces did you pick up?"*
>
> *"Twelve," they replied.*

> "And when I broke the seven loaves for the four thousand, how many basketfuls of pieces did you pick up?"
> They answered, "Seven."
> He said to them, "Do you still not understand?"
> —Mark 8:17-21

When Jesus fed the crowd just before this scene, it wasn't like the disciples were asleep or were merely bystanders. They gave out the fish and bread with their own hands. If anybody should have had an idea of what had happened, they should have! But they still didn't get it. My point is that leaders shouldn't get too exasperated when their people are slow to get on board with a new vision and strategy. In fact, if they get on too easily, it may be a sign that the vision isn't big enough.

Many people in our churches (and on our Leadership Teams) try to avoid chaos at all costs, and they feel confused (and maybe betrayed) when we lead in a way that shakes things up and makes them feel uncomfortable. They want to manage their slice of the organization and tie up all the loose ends, but leaders have a very different agenda: moving the church into the unknown to accomplish a far bigger purpose—and that purpose is more important than maintaining comfort and certainty. I've written and spoken extensively on this subject. For instance, in *Bigger, Faster Leadership*, I commented:

> *Tension points are the places where opposite forces are at work, where flexibility is essential, and in animate objects, where growth happens. Every physical thing in the universe has tension points, and organizations can only grow and thrive if we recognize them and use them appropriately. Trying to avoid them weakens the system and*

ultimately leads to a collapse—sometimes quickly and sometimes slowly.[1]

Of course, chaos is malleable—it's an instrument for good or ill, depending on its purpose. When leaders communicate a vision, strategy, and plan to accomplish something noble and good, it summons the best efforts of everyone involved. However, many people are afraid of chaos because they've been around people who didn't use it for good purposes. They felt used . . . and maybe unsafe. Or perhaps they're afraid to risk any failure. Our job as leaders is to patiently and tenaciously communicate the vision, so people embrace it. Then, and only then, will they support leaders who know that a measure of chaos is absolutely essential for growth.

This means leaders need to recruit, hire, place, and train team members who grasp the importance of productive chaos in the organization. Sometimes, leaders realize one or more of the people on their teams isn't a good fit because they're too resistant. More often, leaders need to retrain or relocate one or more people on the Leadership Team. They can't settle, though, for anything less than thoughtful, eager support for the leader and the vision. In *Who's Holding Your Ladder*, I included a synopsis of five qualities I need in people on my team:

1) **Strength.** They have to be people who can handle instruction and constructive criticism.
2) **Attentiveness.** They ought to be alert to what I'm saying and absorb it quickly. I don't want to give them the same lessons repeatedly.

---

1 Sam Chand, *Bigger, Faster Leadership* (Nashville: Thomas Nelson, 2017), 153.

3) **Faithfulness.** They must have faith in me as their leader and be committed to our shared vision—if they aren't committed to the same vision I am, they'll abandon me.

4) **Firmness.** They must have backbone, so manipulative people won't be able to exploit them.

5) **Loyalty.** They don't always have to agree with me. It's perfectly fine to disagree with my head but not my heart; they may disagree with *how* I do things but not *why* I do them; and they may disagree with my methods but not my motivations.[2]

LEADERS need to recruit, hire, place, and train team members who grasp the importance of productive chaos in the organization.

How do you know if someone on the team refuses to support you? Jesus gave a short parable about people who are too resistant: "Do not give dogs what is sacred; do not throw your pearls to pigs. If you do, they may trample them under their feet, and turn and tear you to pieces" (Matthew 7:6). He was saying that some people can't or won't see the value of the vision and strategy, the what and the why. They aren't just slow to get it; they're defiant and try to lead a revolt against you! They often cloak their resistance in more acceptable language, such as, "Let's get a second opinion," "We should form a task force to consider this idea," or "There will be a better time for this. How about next month?" Leaders

---

2 Sam Chand, *Who's Holding Your Ladder?* (Highland Park, IL: Mall Publishing, 2003), 34.

know that at some point, it's time to fish or cut bait. Delay, for any reason, is no longer an option. Yes, patience and persistence are important, but there's a limit. Leaders want all of their people to understand and support the new vision, but some never will. If these leaders don't have the wisdom and courage to make personnel decisions, resistant people will be anchors holding back the leader, the team, and the church.

I opened this chapter by saying that some leaders were lions who have become overgrown house cats. In other words, lions are convinced that a measure of chaos is essential to organizational health and growth. If they buckle under the pressure to manage and reduce chaos, they abdicate their God-given responsibility to lead with boldness, wisdom, and courage.

DEVELOPING THE TEAM

Countless books have been written on leading teams, and I've contributed to that list myself. There are many good principles to apply, but one is paramount: when trust is built, amazing things can happen; when it's not present, even successes are a grind. When people on a team trust each other, they give the benefit of the doubt about the person's ideas and motives. They can push back on suggestions and plans without being offensive or taking offense, and even their disagreements build more trust because they disagree agreeably. My definition of trust is "a feeling based on repeated realities"; it is built over time with positive experiences, but it can be eroded over time with repeated negative experiences . . . or shattered in an instant by betrayal or abuse. Every interaction makes a difference; none are neutral. Every point of contact either adds to the trust account or becomes a trust tax that reduces the account.

Many Pastors and other leaders believe meetings are the venue where they build trust, but that seldom happens. In meetings, we manage projects, people, and events. We build trust in the meeting *before* the meeting and the meeting *after* the meeting when we meet with people individually. We lead privately and manage publicly. In fact, the meeting before the meeting is the most important, the meeting after the meeting is second in importance, and the meeting itself is least important. If we're not investing our time, energy, and heart in individual conversations before and after a meeting, we're only disseminating information in the meeting—we're not building trust.

The conversations before and after add to our trust account with those people, and we cash it in when we have the meeting with the team. Trust doesn't eliminate challenges, but it oils the machinery, so relationships grow stronger in the midst of difficulties. In his excellent book *The Speed of Trust*, Stephen Covey comments:

> I know it is possible not only to restore trust but to actually enhance it. The difficult things that we go through with the important people in our lives can become fertile ground for the growth of enduring trust—trust that is actually stronger because it's been tested and proved through challenge.[3]

When the trust account is full, leaders can afford to take significant risks with a far bigger vision than ever before. At one point when I was president of the Bible college, we had

---

3 Stephen Covey, *The Speed of Trust* (New York: Simon & Schuster, 2018), 326.

day classes and evening classes, but I was there only during the days. One Friday evening, however, I had to go to my office. When I arrived, I couldn't find a single parking place. I drove down the street, but cars were parked on both sides of the street, one after the other, for half a mile. Finally, I found a spot, and on my way back to the campus, I had an idea: The students who attended classes in the evenings had worked all day, and they were very dedicated to their education. I wondered if a contingent of them would prefer to come to class *before* work each morning.

WHEN the trust account is full, leaders can afford to take significant risks with a far bigger vision than ever before.

On Monday morning, I told Jim, our academic dean, what I'd experienced on Friday night, and I told him my idea about holding classes at six o'clock in the morning. Instantly, he roared with laughter! Jim and I had been friends for years, and we enjoyed working together. For both of us, the trust accounts were full and overflowing. I smiled and asked, "Jim, what's so funny?"

He replied, "Sam, I don't think we could find a single instructor to come for a class that early in the morning!" He paused for a second, and then he continued, "Even if a few students would come, we won't find any professors to get up at 4:30 a.m. and commute into campus for a six o'clock class. It just won't happen."

I didn't give an inch. "Not only do we need teachers. We need our *very best* teachers for the morning classes! And we'll pay them more for teaching those mornings."

He looked intently at me, and he finally realized I wasn't kidding. And by then, he knew I was going to do it with him or without him. He could get on the train or stay at the station, but the train was leaving. I could tell he was willing to join me. I said, "Jim, I want you to schedule three early morning classes for next semester, and find the best teachers for them. We'll see how it goes. If it's a success, we'll expand the number of classes we offer. If it's a bomb, we'll close the book on the idea."

Jim was willing to join me in this venture, but just barely. He shrugged his shoulders and said, "If that's what you want me to do...." I nodded, and he had his marching orders.

When registration opened for the next semester, the three early classes filled up very quickly. As the semester began, a number of the early risers stopped by my office after class to thank me for scheduling them. Two semesters later, the early classes were a staple of our curriculum. But then I noticed something else: Our day classes ended at 1:00 p.m. Our evening classes started at 6:00 p.m. I went to Jim and said, "We're heating and cooling our classrooms when no students are here. Let's schedule some afternoon classes and see what happens." He knew better than to push back this time.

The next semester, we started classes at six o'clock each morning and finished at ten o'clock each night, and there were classes all during the day. Each of these decisions created chaos for every member of our faculty and staff: We needed personnel for financial aid and other resources in our offices during the entire time, we had shifts for janitors, and we had to find adequate parking for students for sixteen hours each day. As we grew our student body, we soon ran out of classrooms. I went to Pastors of local churches and asked if they'd be willing to host a class or two, and they were thrilled to partner with us. Of course, this network built relationships and credibility with church leaders and prospective students throughout the area. By the time I left Beulah Heights in 2003, we had classes in twenty-six locations in Metro Atlanta ... and the students kept coming. In fact, on day one of registration, students came at 4:00 a.m. to be near the front of the line to sign up for classes when we opened the doors at 7:00 a.m. (This was in the era before people were able to register for classes online.)

Every innovative idea creates chaos. A few people eagerly and immediately join us, but most want to probe, ask more questions, and be convinced before they take even a tentative step to get on board. Over the years, I've realized that it's not so important that the people I lead get *it*, but it's monumentally important that they get *me*—how I think, what I value, and how I make decisions. If trust thrives, a world of possibilities opens in front of us.

EVERY innovative idea creates chaos.

If you're a leader, don't let yourself become an overgrown house cat. Remain a lion. Stability may be the goal of a manager, but it's not your friend! Don't be afraid to create some chaos, but make sure it's the good kind.

And if you're a leader, do whatever it takes to build trust with your team, your Board, and everyone else in your orbit. Even if they don't yet grasp your vision and your strategy, they'll give you the benefit of the doubt and support you along the way.

At the end of each chapter, you'll find some questions designed to promote reflection and stimulate discussion with the people on your team or Board. Take plenty of time to consider them. The effectiveness of your leadership may depend on what you find in these discussions.

Father, make of me a crisis man. Bring those I contact to decision.
Let me not be a milepost on a single road; make me a fork, that
men must turn one way or another on facing Christ in me.
—Jim Elliot

CONSIDER THIS:

1) What are some reasons visionary leaders (lions) might become timid and complacent (overgrown house cats)?
2) What are some examples of unexpected chaos that you've used to build relationships?
3) How would you describe the differences between leaders and managers?
4) On a scale of 0 (not in the least) to 10 (all day, every day), how comfortable are you in creating some chaos by casting a big vision and implementing a bold strategy? Explain your answer.
5) What benefits would you experience by being more intentional in having meetings before and after your meetings?
6) What do you hope to get out of this book?

CHAPTER 2

NOT A NEW IDEA

David was the last one we would have chosen to fight the giant, but he was chosen of God.

—Dwight L. Moody

We're all familiar with the day Martin Luther nailed his Ninety-Five Theses to the church door at Wittenberg—which wasn't as dramatic as it sounds... it was like sending an email to everyone in his address book—launching the Protestant Reformation, but we may not grasp the events that led up to this historic moment. The chaos he created has revolutionized the world and has had a profound impact far beyond religious institutions. Luther was born in 1483 in Eisleben, Germany, about 120 miles southwest of Berlin. The family soon moved to Mansfeld, where his father worked in the copper mines. In those days, the dark forests of Germany produced many haunting tales of witches and wolves eager to devour unsuspecting children. Demonic powers seemed to lurk behind every tree, but Luther got no comfort from his stern and demanding father, who regularly beat the boy for the slightest infraction.

When Martin was only thirteen, his father sent him to study law at the University of Erfurt, where he earned two degrees in the shortest time allowed by the university. He was a brilliant scholar, and he was so skilled in debate that he was called "The Philosopher." As a young man of twenty-one, he was caught in a terrifying thunderstorm, and he was almost struck by a bolt of lightning. He called out, "Help me, St. Anne! I will become a monk!"

THE CHAOS Martin Luther's Ninety-Five Theses
created has revolutionized the world and had a
profound impact far beyond religious institutions.

He survived the storm, and true to his word, Luther gave away everything he owned and entered a monastery. He was, perhaps, one of the most dedicated monks in church history. He spent hours in prayer, fasted for long periods, and denied himself creature comforts, enduring the bitter German winters without a blanket, and whipping himself, so he could identify with the scourging of Christ. He hoped these activities and his zeal would draw out the love of God for him. Instead, he grew increasingly frightened of God's righteous wrath. He reflected, "When it is touched by this passing inundation of the eternal, the soul feels and drinks nothing but eternal punishment."[4] Psychologists have connected Luther's fear of God with his relationship with his stern, unaffectionate father, but whatever the cause, Luther's intense dedication produced no comfort, peace, or joy.

In 1510, Luther traveled to Rome to represent his monastery in a dispute at the Vatican. He walked the entire way across the Alps and into Italy, and when he caught sight of the city, he exclaimed, "Be greeted, thou holy Rome, truly holy because of the holy martyrs, dripping with their blood." Like all visitors, he toured the churches, shrines, and other places of interest. But as he explored the city, he saw the grandeur of the homes of powerful members of the Curia, the Catholic senate, and

---

4 "Martin Luther: Passionate Reformer," *Christian History*, 8 Aug. 2008, https://www.christianitytoday.com/history/people/theologians/martin-luther.html.

he heard sordid stories of their blatant immorality. It had only been a few years since Pope Alexander VI, the Borgia pope, fathered numerous children by his mistresses. One such mistress, Lucrezia, was his own daughter, and she, too, bore him a child. When Lucrezia had an affair with the papal chamberlain, her brother reportedly murdered her lover—not to defend her honor but from incestuous jealousy.[5]

In stark contrast to this corruption, Luther climbed the church steps at St. John Lateran on his knees, repeating the Lord's Prayer on every step, with the purpose of freeing his grandfather from purgatory. At the top, however, his doubts clouded any hint of faith.

Only a few years later, Pope Julius was in the middle of one of the largest building projects of the Middle Ages: building a new, monumentally large St. Peter's Basilica. The "mother church" was enormously expensive, and to raise money, Julius sent priests to sell indulgences to reduce the time in purgatory for loved ones. The priest sent to Luther's part of Germany was Johann Tetzel, who preached, "Once a coin into the coffer clings, a soul from purgatory heavenward springs!"

Luther's experience in Rome left him with no illusions about the pope's real motive. Indulgences weren't designed to give comfort to the dead or the living—they were meant to raise money from the poor to build a temple for the rich. Luther defied the pope and his emissary Tetzel by posting his Ninety-Five Theses in 1517, calling the pope's authority into question and denying the value of indulgences.

---

5 Constance Craig Smith, "With Incest, Orgies and Murder Rife, the Borgias Were a Most Unholy Mob," *Daily Mail Online*, 14 June 2019, https://www.dailymail.co.uk/home/books/article-7138775/With-incest-orgies-murder-rife-Borgias-unholy-mob.html.

Not surprisingly, Luther's bold stand set off a firestorm of controversy. Priests, princes, and laymen chose sides—for Luther's truth or against his heresy. Gradually, Luther's position was expanded and strengthened. He taught that righteousness doesn't come through good works but only by faith. This perspective galvanized his followers, and it infuriated his detractors. His break with the church became unavoidable. In 1521, he was ordered to appear before Charles V, the Holy Roman Emperor, in Worms, for yet another debate on his beliefs of *sola fides, sola gratia, sola scriptura*—"Faith alone, grace alone, Scripture alone." He was excommunicated, but he escaped the fate of so many others, who had been burned at the stake, when an allied nobleman sent his soldiers to carry him to a safe hiding place. There, Luther wrote some of the most important works in history. He translated the Bible into German, so common people could read it, and he taught that every vocation is God's high calling which gives every form of work divine dignity.

WHILE Luther's track record is checkered …his elevation of every career has given meaning to even the most humble tasks.

To be honest, his track record is checkered. He wrote and taught ethnic bigotry that hasn't stood up to the scrutiny of time, and he picked fights with other reformers. They had chosen to be on his side in the larger battle for grace and truth, but they differed from him on relatively minor matters. Today, all Protestant denominations trace their roots to Luther. His view of grace, faith, and the Scriptures has formed the bedrock of our theology and practice, and his elevation of every career has given meaning to even the most humble tasks. One scholar sums up Luther's struggle of faith:

> *What seems to* characterize *him more than anything else is an almost childlike trust in God's overarching forgiveness and acceptance. Luther talked much about his tentationes ("temptations"), by which he meant his doubts about whether this divine forgiveness was real. But he overcame these doubts, and his life thereafter was one of joyous and spontaneous trust in God's love and goodness toward him and all sinners. Luther called this "Christian freedom."*[6]

Today, his legacy is found in virtually every country on the planet among an estimated one billion Protestants. Luther was a man whose personality, background, and experiences gave him a fire that couldn't be quenched, and he used that fire to produce theological and ecclesiastical chaos that has reverberated through the centuries.

CHAOS IN THE BIBLE
Abraham

After the human project got off track in the Garden of Eden, the story continued to take dark turns with Cain murdering his brother, Abel, the nations rebelling against God at the Tower of Babel, and God wiping out every person, except one family, in a cataclysmic flood. Things didn't look good for people who were originally created "in the image of God"! But God had plans to put humanity back on track. He picked a man

6 Hans J. Hillerbrand, "Martin Luther: German Religious Leader," *Encyclopædia Britannica*, 22 Aug. 2022, https://www.britannica.com/biography/Martin-Luther.

named Abram (later Abraham) to launch His rescue mission, but God's instructions weren't what we would expect. God promised to make Abraham into "a great nation" and "all peoples on earth will be blessed through you" (Genesis 12:2-3). But there was a problem: Abram and his wife were far beyond childbearing age, and God wasn't exactly forthcoming with detailed instructions. In effect, God said, "Leave your home, and go from here," and Abram responded, "Okay, but where?" God told him, "I'll tell you later." God promised Abram would be the father of a great nation. Abram wondered, *How?* And God told him, "You'll find out later." God promised Abram a homeland. Abram could have asked, "What are the directions?" But God said, "I'll let you know. Just trust Me."

The size of the vision God gave Abram would normally have produced a grand strategy and specific planning, but as the years went by and there was no child, Abram lived in the midst of spiritual and relational chaos—made exponentially worse when he followed his wife's bad advice and fathered a child by her maid! As the couple got older, the tension between faith and despair grew stronger. At one point, Abram gave up on God's promise and chose his nephew as his heir. God assured him, "Do not be afraid, Abram. I am your shield, your very great reward" (Genesis 15:1). God told him to look up at the night sky, and again God promised, "Count the stars— if indeed you can count them. So shall your offspring be" (v. 5). Still, Abram wasn't convinced. He doubted God, and he doubted himself. He asked, "Sovereign Lord, how can I know that I will gain possession of it?" At that moment, we find one of the most unusual and wonderful scenes in all of history.

God told Abram to bring some animals and sacrifice them, forming an aisle between the pieces. Abram instantly knew what this meant; it was the way covenants were made in those days. The one who walked between the pieces was saying, "Let me be cut to pieces if I don't fulfill my part in the covenant," and it was always the lesser, not the greater, who walked down the aisle. But that night, something strange happened. Abram fell into a deep sleep, and "a dreadful darkness came over him." When the sun had set, "a smoking firepot with a blazing torch appeared and passed between the pieces." This was an image of the same kind of fire that appeared on Mt. Sinai years later when God appeared and gave Moses the commandments on tablets of stone . . . and now it was God who was passing between the pieces! God was saying, "I'm not asking you to make this commitment. I'm making it. It's my covenant with you, and I'll fulfill it. If you don't fulfill your part, I'll be torn apart." Again, God promised the land to Abram and his descendants.

In all of the internal doubts and relational tension caused by following God's directions for twenty-five years, Abram desperately needed some reassurance. That fateful day, God appeared in the form of fire and smoke, just like on Sinai and just like in the wilderness over the tabernacle. This scene reminds us that God fulfilled His part of the covenant when He, in the form of Jesus, was torn apart for us because we couldn't keep our part of the covenant. And His last words on the cross were, "Paid in full."

After Isaac was born, it would be logical to assume the chaos was finally over. Not so fast. When the boy was twelve, God saw that the son had pushed Him out of His rightful, central place in Abraham's heart, so He commanded the old man to take his son to Mt. Moriah and sacrifice him. If there has ever been pure chaos in a man's heart, this must have been it. At the last second, as Abraham raised the knife, God stopped him. (Imagine the conversation on the way back down the mountain!) Again, this scene takes us to the cross, where God was willing to sacrifice His Son for our sake, and His heart was just as broken as Abraham's.

Abraham is known as "the father of our faith," but he had to endure decades of chaos to fulfill God's purpose for him.

ABRAHAM is known as "the father of our faith," but he had to endure decades of chaos to fulfill God's purpose for him.

David

David's youthful courage saved King Saul and his army when the young man walked out on the field for individual combat with Goliath, but he probably didn't expect the chaos his new fame would produce when Saul became murderously jealous. On the other side, David created self-inflicted chaos when he committed adultery with his soldier's wife, had him killed in battle, and then lied to cover it up. Still, he repented and was known as "a man after God's own heart."

Nehemiah

Nehemiah created chaos when he launched a bold plan to rebuild the walls of Jerusalem after the Babylonians had destroyed the city and the temple decades before. He faced opposition inside from the Jewish nobles and outside from Sanballat and Tobias. With remarkable leadership skills, he marshaled his workers to complete the wall in only fifty-two days.

Jeremiah

Jeremiah was given an almost impossible task. He rebuked the people and their leaders for their disobedience to God, calling them "broken cisterns that cannot hold water" (Jeremiah 2:13). His fierce denunciations, however, were combined with a tender heart, and he was known as "the weeping prophet." After the people were carried into exile in Babylon, the false prophet Hananiah told the people what they wanted to hear: the exile would be over in two years. But God instructed Jeremiah to give them some very different news, "No, it's going to be seventy years." He continued:

> Build houses and settle down; plant gardens and eat what they produce. Marry and have sons and daughters; find wives for your sons and give your daughters in marriage so that they too may have sons and daughters. Increase in number there; do not decrease. Also, seek the peace and prosperity of the city to which I have carried you into exile. Pray to the Lord for it, because if it prospers, you too will prosper. —Jeremiah 29:5-7

And by the way, "Hananiah will die because he misrepresented Me." A few months later, Hananiah died.

In our time of relative biblical illiteracy and social media misinformation, false prophets like Hananiah tell people what they want to hear . . . about every conceivable topic. Jeremiah is our example of how to be strong, wise, and clear during a national time of chaos and in the face of fierce opposition.

John the Baptist

John the Baptist didn't settle for a comfortable life with his family. He answered God's call to be the "voice crying in the wilderness" to make way for the Messiah. The religious leaders held immense power; they were the civil and spiritual leaders, all rolled into one. But John didn't soft-pedal his message to them:

"You brood of vipers! Who warned you to flee from the coming wrath? Produce fruit in keeping with repentance. And do not think you can say to yourselves, 'We have Abraham as our father.' I tell you that out of these stones God can raise up children for Abraham. The ax is already at the root of the trees, and every tree that does not produce good fruit will be cut down and thrown into the fire."
—Matthew 3:7-10

John, though, suffered from the chaos of unfulfilled expectations. He thought that when the Messiah showed up, He would inaugurate His kingdom, kick the Romans out of Palestine, and rule with righteousness and justice. But when he looked at the impact of Jesus, he didn't see these things happening. When he was in prison for calling out Herod Antipas for adultery, he sent some of his disciples to Jesus to ask, "Are you the one who is to come, or should we expect someone else?" (Matthew 11:3) We need to understand the weight of this simple question. John was asking, "Did I miss the boat? Did I waste my life? You're not what I expected, and I need some help to understand what's going on!"

Jesus told the men:

> "Go back and report to John what you hear and see: The blind receive sight, the lame walk, those who have leprosy are cleansed, the deaf hear, the dead are raised, and the good news is proclaimed to the poor. Blessed is anyone who does not stumble on account of me." —Matthew 11:4-6

These are all characteristics of the Messiah predicted by Isaiah. The kingdom, Jesus was saying to John (and to us), doesn't resolve all the chaos now. Someday, in the new heavens and new earth, every wrong will be made right, but until then, we live in the tension between "the already" and "the not yet."

THE COMING of Jesus' kingdom doesn't resolve all the chaos now. Someday, in the new heavens and new earth, every wrong will be made right, but until then, we live in the tension between "the already" and "the not yet."

LIONS UNTAMED
Jan Hus

Church history is checkered because flawed people have tried to represent Christ, but some have been lions even in the face of intense opposition. Jan Hus lived more than a century before Luther, and his teaching about grace was an early beacon of light for later Protestants. Influenced by John Wycliffe, Hus began to revere the Scriptures above church traditions and practices, "desiring to hold, believe, and assert whatever is contained in them as long as I have breath in me."[7] In his opposition to the pope and church leaders, he was excommunicated, but he continued to preach the gospel of grace.

The pope asked him to attend the Council of Constance to defend his views, and he promised safe passage. However, as soon as Hus arrived, he was arrested and imprisoned. He was brought before the council and tried, but he refused to back away from his faith. He told his inquisitors, "I would not for a chapel of gold retreat from the truth!" On July 6, 1415, he was burned at the stake, singing psalms as he was consumed by the flames. When Martin Luther read a volume of Hus's sermons, he wrote about his surprise: "I was overwhelmed with astonishment. I could not understand for what cause they had burnt so great a man, who explained the Scriptures with so much gravity and skill."[8]

Robert Jermain Thomas

Robert Jermain Thomas lived in the middle of the nineteenth century. Even as a child, he felt called to the mission field. He completed his studies and got married, and the couple moved to Shanghai, China, in 1863. The conditions were unsanitary, so Robert left home to look for other accommodations. While he was away, his wife, who was pregnant, had a miscarriage and died. Robert was emotionally distraught and resigned from his mission agency. He moved to another city in China near its border with Korea where he worked as a customs officer. There, he met other missionaries who

---

7 "John Huss: Pre Reformation Reformer," *Christian History*, 8 Aug. 2008, https://www.christianitytoday.com/history/people/martyrs/john-huss.html.
8 "John Huss: Pre Reformation Reformer," *Christian History*.

introduced him to two Korean Catholics who were part of an underground church.

"The Hermit Kingdom" allowed no contact with foreigners and considered the distribution of literature, including Bibles, to be a crime punishable by decapitation for the distributor and the recipient. Thomas wasn't scared by this fact. He secured crates of Chinese Bibles, but when he entered the country, only a few Koreans would accept copies of the Scriptures. He returned to China with a better understanding of the Koreans' resistance to his faith. At this point, in 1866, Korea began persecuting the underground church, killing more than eight thousand people. Undeterred, Thomas found an American ship going back to Korea, traveling up a river to Pyongyang. Angry Koreans threatened the ship, and in an attempt to escape, it ran aground. The outraged Koreans set their own boats on fire and pushed them into the American vessel, burning it at the water's edge.

According to people on the beach, Thomas grabbed an armload of Bibles and waded ashore. He was killed as he begged people to take copies. A few of those on the beach took copies of the Bible home, not knowing what it was. A government edict demanded the return of all copies for destruction, but one man, a government official named Pak Yong-Sik, decided to use the pages to wallpaper his home. Many friends and visitors read the words, sparking interest in the God of the Bible, on his walls. Miraculously, many Koreans began to believe in Christ. In 1907, a revival swept across the Korean peninsula, and today, more than a quarter of Koreans believe in

Christ. On the beach where Thomas died is the Robert Jermain Thomas Memorial Church.[9]

Thomas's courage didn't protect him from chaos with his wife and child, and it didn't prevent him from being martyred for his faith. The chaos he caused on the beach that day looked like a colossal failure, but God used it to bring a nation to Christ.

Martin Luther King Jr.

American history is indelibly marked with the stain of slavery. Historians estimate that seven hundred thousand people died in the war to end "the peculiar institution," but sadly, the conflict's death and destruction didn't end racism. Soon after the war ended, Reconstruction offered the promise of full citizenship and economic advancement for Blacks, but when it ended, Black Codes and Jim Crow laws severely limited freedom for the previously enslaved, and shockingly, over four thousand Blacks were lynched. In 1948, President Truman issued an executive order ending discrimination in the United States military. In the middle decades of the twentieth century, civil rights legislation was proposed several times, but a powerful Southern block of senators stopped it each time. By the 1950s and early '60s, Black leaders in the South began to call for substantive change. On December 1, 1955, Rosa Parks refused to give up her seat to a White passenger on a Montgomery, Alabama, bus. She was arrested, and the Black community launched the Montgomery Improvement Association, led by a Baptist Pastor, Martin Luther King Jr. A bus boycott

---

9 Simonetta Carr, "Robert Jermain Thomas – First Protestant Martyr in Korea," *Place For Truth*, 27 Apr. 2021, https://www.placefortruth.org/blog/robert-jermain-thomas-first-protestant-martyr-in-korea.

lasted 381 days until the Supreme Court ruled segregation on public transit was unconstitutional.

Two years later, nine Black students tried to attend Central High School in Little Rock, Arkansas, but the children were met by an angry mob and the National Guard called out by Governor Orval Faubus. In 1960, four Black college students had the courage to sit at a Woolworth's lunch counter in Greensboro, North Carolina. For days, hundreds of other students in the South joined them at local stores, and finally, the business owners allowed the original four to be served. It was a significant victory. Momentum for equality and integration increased, and the following year, seven Black and six White people got on a Greyhound bus and became "Freedom Riders" across the South. They faced beatings and bombings from police and bystanders. In Anniston, Alabama, a firebomb was thrown into the bus, and the news covered the scene. The company couldn't find another driver, but United States Attorney General Robert Kennedy forced Alabama Governor John Patterson to find someone to drive another bus for the thirteen Freedom Riders. The violence continued. They were attacked in Montgomery, and the brutality was only stopped by federal marshals. In Jackson, Mississippi, the riders were supported by hundreds of people, and the entire group was arrested for trespassing at a "Whites only" facility.

By April of 1963, Rev. King had drawn national attention. In Birmingham, Alabama, Police Chief Bull Connor turned fire hoses and dogs on protesters, including school children. King hoped for the support of all Black and sympathetic White Pastors, but many of them thought his efforts were doing more harm than good. He was creating chaos, and they couldn't take it. They hoped for a more reasoned, slower, peaceful process of change. When King was arrested, he wrote a letter to the leaders who were hesitant to stand strong for change. The long and impassioned letter contains gems of insight and courage, including:

> "Shallow understanding from people of good will is more frustrating than absolute misunderstanding from people of ill will. Lukewarm acceptance is much more bewildering than outright rejection."

> "So the question is not whether we will be extremists, but what kind of extremists we will be. Will we be extremists for hate or for love? Will we be extremists for the preservation of injustice or for the extension of justice?"

> "Let us all hope that the dark clouds of racial prejudice will soon pass away and the deep fog of misunderstanding will be lifted from our fear-drenched communities, and in some not too distant tomorrow the radiant stars of love and brotherhood will shine over our great nation with all their scintillating beauty."

> "The judgment of God is upon the church as never before. If today's church does not recapture the sacrificial spirit of the early church, it will lose its authenticity, forfeit the loyalty of millions, and be dismissed as an irrelevant social club with no meaning for the twentieth century."

> "Whenever the early Christians entered a town, the people in power became disturbed and immediately sought to convict the Christians for being 'disturbers of the peace' and 'outside agitators.' But the Christians pressed on, in the conviction that they were 'a colony of heaven,' called to obey God rather than man. Small in number, they were

*big in commitment. They were too God-intoxicated to be
'astronomically intimidated.' By their effort and example
they brought an end to such ancient evils as infanticide and
gladiatorial contests."*

In August of 1963, civil rights activists held the March on
Washington, attended by more than two hundred thousand
people, where Dr. King gave his famous speech, "I Have a
Dream." President Lyndon Johnson used his political capital to pass the Civil Rights Act of 1964, guaranteeing equal
employment, ensuring the integration of public places, and
restricting the use of literacy tests for voting. It was a major
step forward, but the fight wasn't over. In the spring of the
following year, as six hundred peaceful people marched from
Selma to Montgomery, they were attacked by Alabama state
and local police under the direction of White supremacist
Governor George Wallace. The day was thereafter known as
"Bloody Sunday."

Dr. King was assassinated on April 4, 1968, on a hotel bal-
cony in Memphis, Tennessee. His death caused an eruption of
anger among Black Americans, as well as Whites who believed
in his cause. Everywhere he went, he created chaos, and he
gave people choices to stand for God's cause of dignity and
love—or superiority and hatred. He was a lion of the Civil
Rights Movement.

EVERYWHERE he went, Martin Luther
King Jr. created chaos, and he gave people
choices to stand for God's cause of dignity
and love—or superiority and hatred. He
was a lion of the Civil Rights Movement.

Nelson Mandela

One of the most remarkable stories from the past few decades is what happened in South Africa. Two men became unlikely partners in turning destructive chaos into something more beautiful than anyone had imagined. Nelson Mandela, the son of a tribal chief, studied law and became one of the country's first Black attorneys. For over a century, the Whites had held Blacks, "coloreds" (a catchall term for people with brown skin whose ancestors are multiracial), and Indians in a second-class status known as *apartheid*. A political activist, Mandela was elected the leader of the youth branch of the African National Congress. At the time, rebel leaders in other countries were amassing armies to fight against oppression and injustice, and Mandela was convinced that armed resistance was the only hope to change racial segregation. He was arrested in 1962 for treason and conspiracy and was sentenced to life in prison and hard labor at the penal colony on Robben Island.

In 1988, Mandela was diagnosed with tuberculosis. At that time, the political landscape was beginning to shift, and less than two years later, he was released from prison. He and President F. W. de Klerk negotiated the end of apartheid, and in 1994, the first time he had been allowed to vote, Mandela was elected president of South Africa.

However, tensions remained high in the country. As a condition of the negotiations over a new constitution, de Klerk insisted on general amnesty for Whites who had committed atrocities. Blacks were still angry about the abuse, police brutality, and inequality that had kept them oppressed and poor for so many decades, and Whites were angry because their place in the culture was no longer supreme. In a brilliant stroke, Mandela and Archbishop Desmond Tutu formed the Truth and Reconciliation Commission. In hearings, victims testified about being tortured and told horror stories about family members who had been murdered or disappeared. But Whites who had suffered from violence committed by the Black liberation movement also testified. Those on both sides who had committed atrocities were given a chance at amnesty, which was only granted if people were transparent and forthcoming about their crimes. The commission received over 7,000 amnesty applications, held 2,500 hearings, and granted amnesty to 1,500 people for their crimes during apartheid.

Reflecting on the importance of the commission's work, Mandela commented, "In the end, reconciliation is a spiritual process, which requires more than just a legal framework. It has to happen in the hearts and minds of people."[10] And Bishop Tutu reflected, "True reconciliation is never cheap, for it is based on forgiveness which is costly. Forgiveness in turn depends on repentance, which has to be based on an acknowledgment of what was done wrong, and therefore on disclosure of the truth. You cannot forgive what you do not know."[11]

And you think you've got problems in your church! These two wise and courageous men (and many others who joined them in this effort) waded into the deeply embedded racial chaos of their country and provided a way for victims and perpetrators to be honest with each other. Each conversation,

---

10 "Address by President Nelson Mandela to the Annual Conference of the Methodist Church," *Nelson Rolihlahla Mandela*, 18 Sep. 1994, http://www.mandela.gov.za/mandela_speeches/1994/940918_methodist.htm.
11 "Statement by Archbishop Desmond Tutu on His Appointment to the Truth and Reconciliation Commission," 30 Nov. 1995, https://www.justice.gov.za/trc/media/pr/1995/p951130a.htm.

each testimony, and each memory of an atrocity—delivered or received—created immediate tension for those involved, but these moments offered healing, hope, understanding, and forgiveness.

Chaos can reinforce our role as lions, or it can reduce us to house cats. Be a lion.

> *A genuine leader is not a searcher for*
> *consensus but a molder of consensus.*
> —Martin Luther King Jr.

CONSIDER THIS:

1) When Luther launched the Reformation, people throughout Europe were plunged into chaos. What were the risks and rewards of taking each side?

2) What are some of your favorite Old Testament characters and accounts that demonstrate courage in the middle of chaos?

3) Reflect on the early days of the church after Pentecost. In what ways did the apostles create chaos? In what ways did they respond to chaos others created?

4) In your life, who, in past decades or currently, is a heroic figure who stepped into chaos and trusted God for something great? How has that person influenced your leadership?

5) What are people saying about you and your leadership? Do they consider you to be a lion or a house cat? Explain your answer.

CHAPTER 3

PLANNED CHAOS OR SURPRISING DISRUPTION?

If we are to better the future we must disturb the present.

—Catherine Booth

As we've seen, chaos can come from a wide variety of sources. In my years as a Pastor and a consultant to Pastors, I've sometimes carefully orchestrated a season of change, but I've also been blindsided by events. Both of these produced chaos, but as you might imagine, one was more challenging than the other.

But let's back up just a bit and examine the inherent questions in the minds of managers and leaders. They have very different responses to chaos and change. Managers ask, "What is?" They focus on the present, the status quo, and the events and people they can control right now. They then ask, "How can we improve this?" They invest their efforts in streamlining and fine-tuning. There's nothing at all wrong with wanting to improve existing systems, but leaders ask very different questions:

"What was?" (looks back at the past)

"What is?" (examines the present)

"What if?" (explores the future)

"Even if?" (helps us count the cost)

The first three are self-descriptive, but the fourth one may need some explanation. When leaders ask themselves and their teams, "Even if?" they're both wondering and determining. They consider going forward with a bold plan even if all the funds aren't in place, even if the timing isn't perfect, even if some team members don't understand, even if some people leave the church, and a thousand other "ifs" that might occur.

When I was the president of the Bible college and had the idea of having classes early in the morning, I asked those questions: "What if we held classes at times when our commuting students might want to come to our school?" "Why wouldn't we give it a try and see what happens?" "The worst that can happen is that students don't sign up for those classes, and we go back to the way things were."

Managers focus on keeping things running; leaders see into the future and create a new reality for their people.

MANAGERS focus on keeping things running; leaders see into the future and create a new reality for their people.

A friend asked me, "Sam, is planned chaos always disruptive?" I answered, "No, it's not. If everyone involved understands completely, tracks with the leader's vision and plan, grasps the what and the why, and fully trusts the leader, there would be no disruption at all."

"But that's not the case in any organization I've ever been in," she told me.

I responded, "Precisely. That's why leaders have to understand the nature of leading into and through chaos to achieve something remarkable. Communicating the what isn't enough. People on the team, on the Board, and in each level of leadership and the church at large need to at least begin to understand the heart, the motives, and the why that propel change and growth."

BLINDSIDED

Unplanned chaos comes in all shapes and sizes, from a natural disaster like a fire or an earthquake to the sudden illness of a team or family member to a recession . . . or a pandemic. None of these has a quick, beneficial outcome. Instead, they usually involve long seasons of restoration and recuperation. But people often grow more from adversity than from unfettered success, so even these calamities can draw people closer, clarify values, and revise a vision.

On April 18, 1906, San Francisco was almost obliterated by a massive earthquake. The shaking lasted only about a minute, but the results were disastrous. Gas lines burst and fires raged for three days, destroying about five hundred city blocks. Half of the city's population of four hundred thousand were now homeless, and about three thousand died in the quake and the fires.[12] A. P. Giannini realized the existing banking system wasn't adequate to provide enough funds to rebuild the city, so he opened a new lending agency, soon called Bank of America. His innovative approach was to lend money directly to the people who needed to rebuild, not just to major developers. Today, his approach is the norm in mortgage lending, but in the summer of 1906 in the Bay Area, it was a startling innovation. In a *Wall Street Journal* article about the need for creative leadership during times of economic and social disruption, Jason Zweig comments about Giannini, "His story shows that

---

12 "San Francisco Earthquake, 1906," *National Archives*, https://www.archives.gov/legislative/features/sf.

innovation often comes when unlikely people and unusual events collide."[13]

During disasters, I believe Pastors and their churches shine most brightly as lights in the darkness. They are salt to preserve people and add flavor to the communities. Again and again, I've seen bold, creative leaders step into dire situations to guide their people as they care for those who have been hurt and displaced. The White House recognizes the crucial role of churches and synagogues. The Office of Faith-Based and Neighborhood Partnerships states, "Nonprofit organizations, including faith-based and community organizations, play a vital role in both preparing for disaster, and in ensuring an inclusive and participatory communitywide recovery from a disaster. These organizations directly supplement and fill gaps where government authority and resources cannot be applied."[14]

Long before government agencies and denominations created organizational arms to respond to emergencies, Christians stepped up and stepped in to help. Some of the most dramatic acts of sacrificial love happened during two devastating plagues in the second and third centuries, each time wiping out about one-fourth of the population of the Roman Empire. The first one was probably smallpox, and the second may have been measles. In each one, the death rate made COVID-19 look like a minor scrape. These were years of severe persecution of Christians, so they had every reason to hide and hope no one blamed them for the diseases, but

13 Jason Zweig, "An Unlikely Hero for 1906, 1929, and Today," *Wall Street Journal*, 29 May 2020, https://www.wsj.com/articles/an-unlikely-hero-for-1906-1929-and-today-11590764100.
14 Justine Brown, "Churches Play a Growing Role in Emergency Management," *Government Technology*, 24 Apr. 2015, https://www.govtech.com/em/disaster/churches-playing-growing-role-emergency-management.html

that wasn't their response. The pagan doctors fled to save their own lives, and many other unbelievers left their family members dying alone in their homes, without even the most basic care of food and water. The Christians, though, didn't run. They stayed, caring for their own who were sick and also for their pagan neighbors. Dionysius, Bishop of Alexandria, described the love and courage of the Christians:

> Most of our brother Christians showed unbounded love and loyalty, never sparing themselves and thinking only of one another. Heedless of danger, they took charge of the sick, attending to their every need and ministering to them in Christ, and with them departed this life serenely happy; for they were infected by others with the disease, drawing on themselves the sickness of their neighbors and cheerfully accepting their pains. Many, in nursing and curing others, transferred their death to themselves and died in their stead.[15]

The sacrifice of the Christians stood in stark contrast to the self-protection of the pagans. Dionysius described the difference:

> But with the heathen everything was quite otherwise. They deserted those who began to be sick, and fled from their dearest friends. They shunned any participation or fellowship with death; which yet, with all their precautions, it was not easy for them to escape.[16]

What difference did this care make? The sick cared for by the Christians had a higher survival rate. Believers exposed themselves to the disease as they provided for their neighbors, and the pagans noticed. At the beginning of the first

---

15 Eusebius, *Eccl. Hist.* 7.22.7–10.
16 Eusebius, *Eccl. Hist.* 7.22.7–10.

plague, Christians counted less than one-tenth of one percent of the empire, but a few decades after the second plague, the church comprised over half of the population. How in the world did this happen? Leaders and their people saw an existential catastrophe and the imminent threat of death as an opportunity to be the hands, feet, and voice of Jesus.

> LEADERS and their people [can make] an existential catastrophe...an opportunity to be the hands, feet, and voice of Jesus.

I've known Pastors of churches that suffered severe damage by natural disasters, such as fires, hurricanes, and earthquakes. Their security was blown and washed away in a matter of hours. But the church building wasn't the only problem; almost every house in these communities experienced damage, from minor to disastrous. It took a lot of time to clean up the rubble, salvage what they could, and begin to rebuild, but through it all, the leaders and their people developed stronger relationships because they experienced shared suffering. Neighbor helped neighbor, whether they were in the church or not. Teams of church members spent days and weeks cleaning up homes, often neglecting their own to care for people down the street or in another neighborhood. Not surprisingly, when services were begun again in a temporary facility, many of these neighbors showed up. The love they felt gave them a hunger to know what motivated the people of the church to care for them.

INTENTIONAL

Thankfully, most of the chaos we experience is intentional, but charting a path into and through significant growth requires wisdom and courage. When I meet with Pastors who want their churches to grow, I want them to invest the time and energy to be 100 percent sure of the what and the why—the strategy behind their vision. The what is easy; the why is much more difficult to get their arms around. I often spend many hours with them, probing and discussing (and often debating) the why. Why this? Why now? Why here? Why these people? Why these benefits? Why this cost?

I'm a safe person who has no personal agenda to get anything from them, so when I push back on an idea, they don't take it personally. No matter how long it takes, we don't move on until the why is crystal clear and compelling. At that point, I ask the three questions that move toward the what: "What if?" "Why not?" and "What's the worst that can happen?"

Then, we develop a communication strategy:

» What do you say to your Leadership Team and your Board to bring them along carefully and patiently so they "get it"?

» When do you cast the vision?

» How do you frame it, so they can understand?

» What's the right sequence of details they need?

» What are the questions you need to anticipate?

» Which of these questions need to be answered before you talk to them, and which ones will be answered along the journey?

Some Pastors jump too quickly to sow the seeds of a vision without preparing the soil. I encourage them to spend time in leadership and Board meetings getting to know each other better, focusing on the relationships, and building trust. They can affirm each other and celebrate all that God has done and is doing among them. (This is very important, so they may need to cultivate these relationships for several months before beginning to share a new vision.) Poor leaders assume they've already created a growth culture, or they're oblivious to the importance of trust, but good leaders carefully cultivate an atmosphere of openness and appreciation. As we've seen, good leaders know that what happens in the meeting is a product of what happened in the meetings before the meeting. Breakfasts, ball games, phone calls, and open-ended conversations work wonders to overcome suspicions and build trust.

As we think about the people we lead and serve, virtually all of us can instantly identify the Leadership Team and Board members who will ask the hardest questions, and we know the one others look to as the weathervane of the group. If they point in the right direction, others will follow, but if not . . . winning them over, or at least, neutralizing their resistance, is an important prerequisite. Then, when the time is right, the leaders can begin to roll out the vision to the rest of the Board and the Leadership Team, which can be framed by the same three questions they've debated with me and themselves. The preparatory conversations will make vision casting much easier, and people will embrace it more readily. People will still have plenty of questions, but leaders will be much farther down the road than if they hadn't created the positive atmosphere.

THE POWER OF STORIES

When we cast a vision, we need to lead with a compelling narrative. People love stories, so give them one that touches their hearts and opens their eyes. For instance, when I had the idea about starting classes early in the morning, I began, "Jim, I was on campus last night, and the parking lots and streets were so packed that I had to park a long way down the street. Women were walking in heels in the street because there's no sidewalk on these streets. As I looked at these people, I wondered what we could do to make life easier and safer for them . . . and I had an idea: we could offer classes early in the morning." My narrative became the picture frame for the vision.

Sometimes, an unexpected opportunity is the cause of chaos. I consulted with a Pastor who called me one day and explained that he was holding a manila envelope containing an offer to buy his church building and property. The offer was for millions of dollars over what he thought it was worth, and the buyer offered generous terms: the church could continue at that location for two years while they found new property and built a new facility. He said, "Sam, I think this is an opportunity we can't pass up, but our people love this place. How can I help them see the benefits of the move?"

SOMETIMES, an unexpected
opportunity is the cause of chaos.

I advised him, "Take plenty of time to research the history of the church over its seventy years, and find specific stories about how God has worked in and through people in the congregation. Talk about hardship and loss, compassion and miraculous provisions, and the impact on families and the community. Find pictures and, more recently, videos of the people who have meant so much to the church. Explain how unlikely the positive outcomes were, but they happened because God's people trusted Him to do the impossible."

I continued on, "Tell stories of bold faith, courageous obedience, and trust in God's love and power. Tell these stories, tell them often, and tell them well. Connect the stories with passages of Scripture when God's people were in big trouble, but leaders trusted Him to show up and pull them through. In fact, these narratives comprise most of the Bible! Abraham, Isaac, and Jacob; Joseph and Gideon; David and Solomon; Elisha and Elijah; Jeremiah and Isaiah; the disciples and Paul, and most of all, Jesus. Each of them faced daunting tests of faith. There were no easy, quick solutions, but they waded into the chaos and trusted God to provide for them . . . and He did. The first seventeen verses of Matthew list the genealogy of Jesus, and it contains some very unexpected characters, including a prostitute, a woman who was a Moabite, and a murderer—and God worked through people like that . . . like the people in your church."

Within a few minutes, he got it. He could visualize himself in the rooms with his Board and his team as he told stories about the church's history of bold faith, and he was sure that these narratives would capture their hearts. And he could then imagine telling the same stories from the platform on Sunday mornings.

The importance of stories as a primary communication tool isn't a new concept. The defining narrative of the Jewish people is God delivering their ancestors from slavery in Egypt, parting the Red Sea, and then leading them for forty years to the Promised Land. Again and again, throughout the Psalms and the prophets, this story reminds them of their God-given identity. The New Testament doesn't drop this story. Instead, it incorporates it into the gospel message: Jesus is the true temple, Jesus is the high priest, Jesus is the perfect sacrifice, and Jesus delivers His people from the slavery of sin and death. The Jews and the early Christians were expert storytellers, and we need to follow their example, so our people will fulfill the vision God has given us.

To be sure, most Pastors are brilliant storytellers on the platform, but they forget to tell stories in the boardroom and in team meetings. Does telling them take time? Yes, but don't we expend far more time and energy trying to get people to buy into our vision when we don't tell them? Yes, we do.

Narratives create momentum which is velocity times mass. Velocity is speed in a given direction. The facts of the stories are the mass, and the emotion generated by the stories is the velocity—together, they create momentum toward a new reality.

NARRATIVES create momentum which is velocity times mass. Velocity is speed in a given direction. The facts of the stories are the mass, and the emotion generated by the stories is the velocity—together, they create momentum toward a new reality.

When the Pastor talked to his leaders about the offer to buy his church, he told them, "In my hand is a fantastic offer to buy our church. I'm afraid to talk to you about it, but I'm not afraid to talk about God's faithfulness over our history to challenge us and provide for us. I believe God wants to do it again. Here. Now. With us. I'm confident because those who came before us, and those who are in this room, have believed God for amazing things. Over and over again, we've seen His faithfulness to lead and provide. Let me tell you about some of these people. . . ." After telling a few stories, he told them, "Now, with trembling hands, I want to pull the papers out of this envelope and let you see the possibility for a new chapter in our story."

When the Pastor read the letter and shared the offer, there was weeping in the room. Not anger, not fear, not distrust. He had admitted his own fear of change, and he shared how people in the church had, for years, overcome their fear with faith. He was very honest with them: "I'm sure you have a lot of questions, but at this moment, I have few answers. I assure you though, that together, we'll explore every detail and resolve every issue—at least as much as we can, because there will always be unknowns in every venture. I'm not asking you to trust me; I'm asking you to trust God. I think we can."

Do not pray for tasks equal to your powers.
Pray for power equal to your tasks.
—Phillips Brooks

CONSIDER THIS:

1) What are some surprising events that have caused chaos in your life and in your church? How did you respond to each one?

2) What is your reaction to the concept of "intentional chaos"? Does it seem thoroughly insane or an essential part of leadership? Explain your answer.

3) Think of "your next good idea" for your ministry, and answer these questions:
   » What was?
   » What is?
   » What if?
   » Even if?

4) What are two or three of your favorite stories in the Bible? What makes them ring in your heart?

5) What are some stories of great faith and God's faithfulness among the unlikely people to be heroes in your church's history?

6) Does your church have archives of any kind? How can you uncover the hidden or forgotten stories? How will you use them? When will you use them? What impact do you think they'll have?

CHAPTER 4

WHEN LEADERS LEAD

It takes more than a busy church, a friendly church, or even an evangelical church to impact a community for Christ. It must be a church ablaze, led by leaders who are ablaze for God.

—Wesley L. Duewel

S iegfried & Roy was one of the most popular acts in Las Vegas, performing an animal-taming act with white lions and white tigers at the Mirage Resort and Casino. Their act was one of the longest in history: forty-four years, before something went terrifyingly wrong. On October 3, 2003, Roy was on stage with Mantacore, a white tiger. From the beginning, the tiger walked away from his marked spot on the stage. Instead of walking the tiger in a circle like he usually did, Roy used his arm to try to steer it, putting the tiger's face directly in his stomach area. Mantacore was confused and reacted violently. Roy tried to calm the animal, but the tiger bit his arm, knocked him to the floor, bit his neck, and carried him backstage like a captured antelope. One person who witnessed the event reported, "It took four men and a fire extinguisher to get the tiger off him." The tiger had bitten through one of Roy's vertebrae, severing an artery to the brain, resulting in a stroke.

In the ambulance on the way to the emergency room, Roy told one of the EMTs, "Mantacore is a great cat. Make sure no harm comes to Mantacore." When it was over, the tiger calmed down and returned to his kennel without further violence.[17]

You'd think this kind of event would give people reason to be more cautious around lions and tigers, but not long ago, as

---

17 Jamie Burton, "Why Mantacore the Tiger Attacked Roy Horn of Siegfried and Roy," *Newsweek*, 18 Jan. 2022, https://www.newsweek.com/why-tiger-attacked-siegfried-roy-explained-1670348.

I was scrolling through Instagram, I noticed a lady petting a tiger's head. The animal's lethal jaws were only a foot from her face. Crazy ... just crazy.

Or maybe not.

THE PETTING ZOO

As I mentioned earlier, leaders are meant to be lions—bold and strong, but not vicious. However, too many have been tamed by years of resistance, disappointment, and self-doubt. Another image that comes to mind is a petting zoo. When my daughters were little, they walked with delight through a menagerie of lambs, kid goats, rabbits, turtles, and other creatures that were no threat at all. These placid animals remind me of Pastors and other leaders who have lost their vision and their zeal to make a difference. They're happy to be petted by nice people who say nice things about nice messages and nice events, and any form of passion for accomplishing anything meaningful looks totally out of place.

I could give many examples, but let me tell you about a woman who started her ministry as a world-changer. When she took a role as a youth Pastor, she had a voracious appetite for leadership principles, and she tried to implement them as soon as she got a good grasp of them. She inspired students, volunteers, and everyone else around her to be more and do more. About five years later, her senior Pastor retired, and the Board called her to become the Pastor. The honeymoon period lasted about six months, but after that, Board members complained that she was moving too fast and asking too much of them. They said her zeal was fine for students, but it didn't work for adults—especially adults who thought they knew more about leadership than she did.

For a year, she wrestled with a crisis of confidence. Didn't God call her to lead with vision and passion? Couldn't she transfer what worked so well with students to the Board and discipling men and women in the church? Some of her efforts to change programs worked, but others flopped. Some of those on her Leadership Team agreed with the Board that she was trying to do too much too soon. Every meeting became an ordeal, and gradually, she settled for the affirmations she could get by preaching nice sermons and not asking too much of anyone. She had been tamed, and she became one of the lambs in the church's petting zoo.

FROM MY DECADES of observing people, I can say with certainty that no one initially plans to be one of the animals in a petting zoo.

From my decades of observing people, I can say with certainty that no one initially plans to be one of the animals in a petting zoo. Men and women who respond to God's call to ministry don't start with the dream of being average. They don't fantasize about getting a housing allowance and some tax breaks. Their minds don't run to the joy of being in boring meetings talking about mundane details. Their highest hopes aren't doing baby dedications or recruiting for special events. No, they show up because they have a deep, God-inspired desire to be agents of change, to make a difference, to reach the lost and stoke the fire of passionate love and obedience in people around them—to change their people, change their communities, and change the world. Nothing less than that.

I know being tamed can easily happen because it happened to me. As I shared in the opening chapter, when I became a Pastor, I met immediate resistance from my Board when I wanted to give our church a little more visibility in the yellow pages, and they weren't finished saying "no" to my ideas. Soon, some people left the church, and whom was that a reflection of? Obviously me. When I prepared sermons, I was sure the message would touch and transform people, but when I spoke, they looked at me like they couldn't wait to go to lunch. When I stood at the door at the end of the service, they shook my hand, smiled, and said, "Thanks, Pastor Sam. That was a really nice message." It was like they were patting me on the head and saying, "We like it when you're a lamb, Pastor Sam. Stay in the petting zoo. I hope it's comfortable for you." Gradually, I concluded that this was the best it could be; I was going to be a pleasant Pastor giving encouraging sermons to people who were content only when they weren't pushed very much. Everybody could be happy in the petting zoo.

I also have consulted with a number of Pastors who still have fire in their souls, but they've redirected it to managing events and people. They want to be the very best managers they can be. There's nothing wrong with wanting to do a job well, but I'm afraid they've redefined their job . . . redefining it down to something less than visionary leadership. They've become doers, not dreamers. They focus on fine-tuning their systems rather than making a difference. They're risk-averse, unwilling to try something without at least a high probability of success.

Instead of changing the world, they want to change how well the church operates, with a vision inside the walls instead of expanding outside into the community. Their game plan is to avoid losing, not winning big. To extend my analogy, they're not exactly animals in the petting zoo, but they're ponies that older kids feel safe riding. These Pastors work hard and strive for excellence, so they're not going to admit they're not lions any longer. This is especially true of Pastors who are in their 60s and looking forward to retirement. They don't want to take too many chances, and they don't want to rock the boat. They just want to keep doing a few things well until the door closes behind them.

Am I being too harsh, too critical of Pastors? I don't think so. When I've talked to them about what I see, almost every one thanks me for reminding them why they went into the ministry in the first place. As we talk, they begin to see their gradual slide from passion to passivity, and they're eager to change the trajectory of their leadership. They know they were called to be lions, not house cats.

A LION'S ROAR

I've had the privilege of knowing some remarkable leaders. Let me list a few characteristics that are common to them:

- » They have a high threshold for risk. They're not afraid to fail, and they don't take failure personally. This gives them a lot of room to experiment and be honest about the results.
- » They applaud team members who show a high risk threshold. They don't insist on being the only ones with great ideas.

» They eagerly soak up the insights and ideas of other gifted leaders, so they're always learning and growing. They know that leaders outside their own ecosystem probably see things through a different lens, and they can learn from those leaders.

» They're emotionally and psychologically secure. Their intensity isn't misplaced in condemning those who fail, and they don't daydream about awards and praise.

» They see failure as a normal part of learning, not a cataclysm.

» They can accept others' disappointment, confusion, and resistance without overreacting.

» They know that all significant ministry is built on the bedrock of trust, which is established by a long history of honest, affirming relationships and a track record of wise decisions.

Not long ago, I met with a friend who is one of the finest leaders I've ever known. He shared some elements of a new vision, but I could tell something was bothering him. I asked, "What's the matter? What are you afraid of?"

He looked at me and replied, "Sam, I'm afraid I'll be too discouraged by my thousandth failure."

He's a leader who isn't surprised by failure. Of course, he tries to be as wise as possible, so he can avoid failure if possible, but the risk of failure is inherent in any grand venture. His comment told me that he was imagining the limits of his risk-taking. What would it take for him to come to the end and give up? If it were five hundred failures, he still had a long way to go!

TO LEAD into and through chaos, leaders need
to make regular deposits of relational equity.

Leadership is sometimes lonely, but a leader is never alone
in the vision. To lead into and through chaos, leaders need
to make regular deposits of relational equity. As we've seen,
these deposits don't happen in Board and Leadership Team
meetings. They happen in unguarded, relaxed times, and
they happen when the leader is honest and vulnerable. If you
don't have enough deposits of trust-building connections,
meetings can become strained, mundane, and sometimes
contentious. Patrick Lencioni has written authoritatively
about the necessity of leaders building trust. He has observed,
"People will walk through fire for a leader that's true and
human." Trust is the most essential ingredient on any team.
Lencioni notes that a culture of trust has a powerfully positive ripple effect:

> The impact of organizational health goes far beyond the
> walls of a company, extending to customers and vendors,
> even to spouses and children. It sends people to work in the
> morning with clarity, hope, and anticipation and brings
> them home at night with a greater sense of accomplish-
> ment, contribution, and self-esteem. The impact of this is
> as important as it is impossible to measure.[18]

---

18 Patrick Lencioni, *The Advantage: Why Organizational Health Trumps Everything Else In
Business* (Hoboken, NJ: John Wiley & Sons, 2016), 193.

ANTICIPATING CHANGE

Leaders know that their people don't see things as clearly as they do. That's the nature of leadership, not a flaw in the followers. In fact, most team members get excited about a big vision . . . until they realize what it demands of them. They may have to change roles and schedules, and they may need to acquire additional skills. When they realize the cost, they may balk at the idea. The leader is the only one who sees the full picture, and even then, parts of it don't come into focus until later in the process. The leader has a bold vision, but it's unreasonable to assume that others can see it right away, and in fact, it's unreasonable to assume the leader can fully explain it from the beginning. Most (if not all) leaders are intuitive. They often sense God's leading before they can articulate it. This thrills a few people around them, but it confuses and terrifies others!

A helpful concept of anticipating the need for change is the Sigmoid Curve. Virtually every organization follows a similar path of start-up with initial struggles, significant growth, stagnation, and decline. The best and smartest leaders anticipate the need to recharge vision before stagnation happens, injecting new ideas and new sources of energy to propel a new upward trajectory.

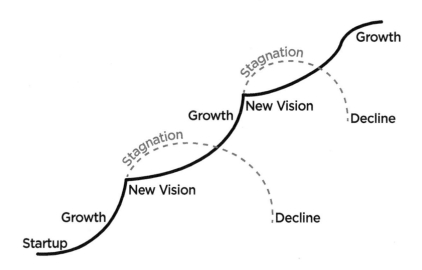

It takes enormous foresight and courage for a leader to shift gears and change directions when everything is going well in the growth stage. People are surprised and ask, "Why start something new? We're doing great!" But the wise leader knows the organization needs a shot of fresh energy *before* they begin to stagnate. If the leader waits until stagnation begins, far more effort will be required to change the trajectory to an upward path. And if she waits until the decline, she may not have the job to right the ship.

IT TAKES enormous foresight and courage for a leader to shift gears and change directions when everything is going well in the growth stage.

Over the years, I've found the concept of the Sigmoid Curve to be incredibly helpful. It warns leaders to avoid being complacent, and it prompts them to lead boldly when they could just coast. Many people will wonder what's going on, so it's important to share the concept of the curve and the rationale behind launching the new vision.

When a Pastor communicates a bold vision, it often galvanizes the commitment of the Board, the team, volunteers, and everyone within earshot. With a mixture of excitement and fear of the unknown, people wake up, sit up, and stand up to be involved. A clearly articulated purpose and plan give people confidence, and they realize they can be part of something much bigger than themselves. It may be a new program, a new building, a new multisite campus, a new method of communication, a new outreach, or something else that captures attention and hearts. But the galvanizing vision may not be something like these at all.

During the pandemic, people at all levels wondered how to respond—to open or not, to require masks or not, and what it means to be people of faith in a time of contagion. Some Pastors preempted the confusion by announcing their churches would be closed for six months, and then they'd reevaluate. They realized that the landscape had instantly become a seascape with rolling waves and changing conditions. In the meantime, they put their energies into online services and encouraged group and team leaders to stay connected with their people on social media platforms and online video meetings. This strategy took a lot of pressure off the Pastor and everyone else to make major decisions week by week, and it allowed them to be creative in continuing the mission using different tactics. Instead of being confused and frustrated with having to make a hard decision every week, they could explore ways of ministry they'd never imagined before.

The building was no longer the center of ministry; now, virtually everything was online. But this brought up another set of questions, such as: How could the worship team be used most effectively? How could messages connect most powerfully? How would people send their offerings? How could children and youth ministries be effective? A lot of new questions had to be asked and answered, and a lot of resources had to be repurposed. These Pastors took a lot of heat, but not from their own people. Other Pastors criticized them for not staying open and "giving in" to the pandemic. But these Pastors clearly articulated the benefits of their decision, and their people felt deeply loved and well-led.

THE MUDDY MIDDLE

No matter how clearly leaders communicate a fresh vision, many of their people will need time, patience, and repetition to understand it. Sometimes, when I meet with Leadership Teams that are trying to get their arms around their Pastor's new vision, I tell them, "I'm going to give you a vocabulary for change, and I'm going to tell you what's going to happen before it happens. At different points, you're going to feel confused and maybe overwhelmed. Know that's coming, so when it happens, accept the feeling without getting upset and blaming other people. In any bold initiative, initial enthusiasm inevitably devolves into a season of drudgery and uncertainty. I call this 'the muddy middle.' If you expect it, you can accept it as part of the process." This brief but important conversation reorients their expectations and gives them shelves where they can put their not-so-positive emotional reactions when their passion has waned, responsibilities are multiplying, and they feel frustrated with the Pastor and others on the team. Instead of sulking and blaming, they can encourage each other during "the muddy middle," which builds trust instead of eroding it.

Jesus knew the beginning and the end of His mission. I'm convinced that one of His chief frustrations was that His disciples couldn't absorb His purpose to be the true and final sacrifice for the sins of the world, even though He told them over and over again. One particular passage shows the glory and the agony. Jesus took the disciples north from the Sea of Galilee to Caesarea Philippi, near Mount Hermon. He asked them, "Who do people say the Son of Man is?"

They replied, "Some say John the Baptist; others say Elijah; and still others, Jeremiah or one of the prophets."

"But what about you?" he asked. "Who do you say I am?"

Simon Peter answered, "You are the Messiah, the Son of the living God."

Jesus replied, "Blessed are you, Simon son of Jonah, for this was not revealed to you by flesh and blood, but by my Father in heaven. And I tell you that you are Peter, and on this rock I will build my church, and the gates of Hades will not overcome it. I will give you the keys of the kingdom of heaven; whatever you bind on earth will be bound in heaven, and whatever you loose on earth will be loosed in heaven." —Matthew 16:13-19

Finally, it seemed that at least Peter got the picture! But not so fast. In the very next scene, Jesus explained that He was going to Jerusalem to be betrayed and killed, but He would rise again on the third day. Peter was all about Jesus being the Messiah because the Jews expected the Messiah to be a military and political leader, just like King David, to drive the Romans out of Palestine and reestablish God's kingdom. A dead Messiah just didn't make any sense to Peter, so he took Jesus aside and said, "Never, Lord! This shall never happen to you!"

Jesus didn't blink. He told Peter, "Get behind me, Satan! You are a stumbling block to me; you do not have in mind the concerns of God, but merely human concerns."

It seems the others must have overheard this exchange because Jesus turned to them to reframe their expectations. They may have wanted Him to be a victorious warrior, but His kingdom would come through sacrifice and suffering, not the sword. I can imagine they were stunned when He explained:

"Whoever wants to be my disciple must deny themselves and take up their cross and follow me. For whoever wants to save their life will lose it, but whoever loses their life for me will find it. What good will it be for someone to gain the whole world, yet forfeit their soul? Or what can anyone give in exchange for their soul? For the Son of Man is going to come in his Father's glory with his angels, and then he will reward each person according to what they have done." (vv. 21-27)

Did they get it then? No, not even close. On the night Jesus served Passover to them, He gave them bread and wine. They may have wondered where the dish of lamb was. The lamb wasn't *on* the table because the Lamb was *at* the table. Even then, they were clueless. Luke tells us that immediately after the Last Supper, the disciples argued about who would be the greatest. I think they still believed Jesus was going to be inaugurated as the conquering king the next day, and they were jockeying for position in His cabinet!

[THE DISCIPLES'] story is a larger version of what all leaders experience on a smaller scale: we try hard to explain where we sense God leading us, and we fill in the details as early as we can, but some of our people just don't get it.

The disciples had a fixed image of what *would* happen and what *should* happen, and they simply couldn't grasp the different reality that Jesus explained so often. This story is a larger version of what all leaders experience on a smaller scale: we try hard to explain where we sense God leading us, and we fill in the details as early as we can, but some of our people just don't get it. If the disciples spent three years, night and day, with Jesus, and they were so dim, we can be a bit more patient with people on our teams who are slow on the uptake.

I wish I'd understood this statement years ago: Just because you see the vision doesn't mean you can articulate and show it clearly. And even when you can articulate it and show it, it doesn't mean your people will grasp it. At every level of leadership we find a "wisdom gap." The Pastor sees the vision most clearly, the Executive Team (or the equivalent in smaller churches) doesn't see it quite as well, and the people who report to them are even a little fuzzier. These gaps proceed all the way down through teams of volunteers and small groups to regular attenders and to the most recent visitor. Unfortunately, I've seen that in many classes for new members, the goal is to welcome people to the petting zoo, to assure them that everyone is nice and harmless. If people have suffered from some kind of abuse from authority figures, that may be exactly the right message, but I believe we severely dampen the enthusiasm of newcomers when we fail to impart a big vision for the church to them.

What does closing the gap look like in actual experience? A Pastor shares a strategic vision, the What? and the Why? with the Executive Team, but they're often geared for tactical implementation, so they ask Who? When? Where? How? and How much? It's crucial, then, to minimize the gap at the top between the Pastor and the Executive Team, so they begin to grasp and share the strategic vision with their teams and then throughout the organization. In other words, focus primarily on the what and the why, and give them language, so they can repeat it to their teams. By the time the vision is communicated at the end of the organizational chart, it will almost certainly be shared as tactics. That's why it's important for the Pastor to regularly communicate—I'd say over-communicate—the vision in church services and in every Leadership Team and Board meeting. As Pastor Andy Stanley observed, "Vision leaks." We need to keep pouring it in to replenish what has leaked out.

Let me make two other points: First, during the process of sharing the strategic vision and helping the Board and team grasp it and begin to make tactical plans, look for people who demonstrate strategic thinking. You probably have one or two people who show some promise to develop their leadership capacity and skills, so they can be more than managers. Notice them, affirm them, and nurture this trait in them. And second, some people may be confused, or even alarmed, that I compare leaders to lions. I would remind these people that Jesus is both the Lamb of God and the Lion of Judah—both, not one or the other.

JESUS IS both the Lamb of God and the Lion of Judah—both, not one or the other.

We have a distorted and limited concept of Him if we don't embrace both sides of His character: limitless power and limitless love. Years ago, Thomas Howard wrote a book titled *Christ the Tiger*; the title is taken from a poem by T. S. Eliot. The book is an autobiographical account of Howard's attempt to hold both traits, Christ's awesome power and limitless love, at the same time. If we see Christ as only the mighty Creator who will come to judge in righteousness, we may be terrified of Him, and if we see only His tender affection, our faith will probably be sentimental but not vibrant. Holding both together—the Lion and the Lamb—expands our faith, deepens our worship, and makes a radical commitment to Him the only reasonable response.[19]

MAYBE, JUST MAYBE

Thankfully, there are many examples of leaders who have seen a need and taken a risk to meet it. They remind me of

---

19 Thomas Howard, *Christ the Tiger* (Eugene, Oregon: Wipf & Stock, 2004).

Jonathan, King Saul's son, when the army was being attacked by the Philistines in 1 Samuel 14:1-20. Saul was in big trouble. Many of the men had deserted, and those who were left had few armor or weapons. Only Saul and Jonathan had swords in hand. The young man and his armorbearer saw a detachment of Philistines. They were alone, but Jonathan told the armorbearer, "Come, let's go over to the outpost of those uncircumcised men. Perhaps the LORD will act in our behalf. Nothing can hinder the LORD from saving, whether by many or by few" (v. 6). They boldly attacked and killed twenty soldiers, and God rewarded their courage by causing an earthquake! The Philistines fled: "It was a panic sent by God" (v. 15). Saul rallied his men to join the fight, and the Philistines were routed. I've always been amazed at Jonathan's brazen courage. He had no promise of success, only a "perhaps," but that was enough to propel him forward.

Today, we find some brave leaders in the spirit of Jonathan. Craig Groeschel was one of the very first Pastors to launch an online service. He invested in the equipment and staff to make it happen, not knowing if it would work. He changed the way church is delivered.

Vashti Murphy McKenzie was the first woman elected as bishop of the African Methodist Episcopal Church and provides leadership to more than two hundred churches. She was appointed by President Obama to serve on the President's Advisory Council of the White House Faith-Based and Neighborhood Partnerships and is the author of five books. In 2015, she was named as one of the fifty most powerful women religious leaders in the world.

Christine Caine and her husband, Nick, saw the plight of human trafficking, but they offered much more than "thoughts and prayers." They launched the A21 Campaign, which won the Mother Theresa Memorial Award for their work to rescue refugees from being trafficked.

Ron Kenoly created a revolution in worship music. A visionary and an artist, he trains and mentors worship leaders around the globe. His influence shaped much of modern worship, including Hillsong, Elevation Worship, and Maverick City.

When Tony Evans was a student at Dallas Theological Seminary, a Houston radio producer contacted a professor to ask if he could provide outstanding preaching for his program. The professor recommended Tony, and his radio career was launched. About ten years later, Evans was a very popular preacher, and requests for copies of his sermons flooded in. At that point, he began The Urban Alternative, a radio program that is broadcast today to millions in more than 130 countries.

Roselen Boerner Faccio has taken a circuitous route to an astounding impact for Christ. An Italian, she trained to become a nun, but she left the Catholic church and started an independent church in Milan. Today, about two decades later, Sabaoth Church is the largest congregation in the city. But Roselen wasn't finished. She has planted fifty-four churches in Italy, Germany, Spain, Brazil, and other countries. Her organization, Hanger 24, is a training school for missionaries, and its outreach programs are quite innovative, including street theater.

Bill Hornsby was one of the founders of ARC, the Association of Related Churches, which has become one of the most effective church-planting organizations. He changed the way churches are planted.

Kathleen Cooke co-founded The Influence Lab to equip and mentor women in entertainment and media, but she doesn't spend all her time with celebrities. Her heart is big enough to be on the national board of the Salvation Army. She cares for those who are up-and-comers and people who are down-and-out.

Chadwick S. Mohan is the Pastor of New Life Assembly of God in Chennai, India, and is instrumental in church-planting efforts throughout the country. He is on the board of Project Rescue, a nonprofit, multinational network dedicated to helping sexually exploited women escape and find dignity and healing.

Chris Hodges created the most powerful and widely used curriculum for discipleship in the church called *Growth Track*. He changed the way disciples are made.

I know a lot of Pastors who have shown just as much creativity, just as much boldness, and just as much faith in being world-changers, regardless of their church's size and location. They've learned to inject enough vision for their people to swallow but not so much that they choke on it. They're making a difference outside the walls of their churches, reaching people who would never come to church unless someone went out of their way to engage them, providing resources for the lost and the least, and being a light shining in the community's darkness.

It's certainly possible to have a bold vision but communicate poorly. Genesis 37:3-11 recounts Joseph was Jacob's favorite son, and the other brothers knew it. He had two dreams about the future of his family and his role in it, but he should have kept his mouth shut. When he told his parents and brothers, it was the wrong message for the wrong audience! The first dream was about his brothers bowing down to him, and they reacted, "Do you intend to reign over us? Will you actually rule us?" (v. 8) And they hated him even more. His second dream included his parents bowing to him. His dad, Jacob, wasn't any happier than the brothers: "What is this dream you had? Will your mother and I and your brothers actually come and bow down to the ground before you?" (v. 10)

The brothers didn't wait long to put Joseph in his place—a deep, dark place. They sold him to a passing caravan and into slavery. Yes, God had a plan for the young man that was fulfilled in his time in Egypt, but we shouldn't overlook the insensitivity and immaturity of his youth.

Leaders need to understand the difference and the relationship between *chronos* and *kairos*: *chronos* is time—sequential, using a clock and a calendar; *kairos* is timing—tailoring the right message to the right people at the right time. We need to bring people along, pushing and pulling them enough to make progress but without going too slow or too fast. We need to be clear communicators.

Don't be too slow, and don't be in a hurry. Don't assume your trust account is full; make deposits before you share your heart and your vision. Farmers don't plant seed without plowing and disking the soil to prepare it. Then they carefully plant the seeds to assure maximum germination and growth. The metaphors in the Scriptures about leadership are primarily farming and shepherding. Both require a future orientation, patience, and persistence. Vision casting is a fine art, one every leader needs to develop. As we've seen, stories are essential. They stimulate the imagination and give people a mental image of what *has* happened, so they can then connect with the vision of what *can* happen.

When leaders lead, God works, and the world is changed.

WHEN LEADERS lead, God works,
and the world is changed.

A true shepherd leads the way. He does not merely point the way.
—Leonard Ravenhill

CONSIDER THIS:

1) Do you think the analogy of the petting zoo is too harsh? Why or why not?
2) How would those who know you well describe your threshold for risks? Do you agree or disagree with that assessment?
3) How do you usually respond to failure? What would be a healthier way to respond?
4) Explain the concept of the Sigmoid Curve in relation to vision casting. Does launching a new initiative during a season of growth seem really odd or really wise? Explain your answer.

5) Describe the "wisdom gap" in the levels of leadership in your church. What are some ways you can close the top gap? How will closing the gap enlist your team as carriers of the vision and help you lead more effectively?

6) Has God put a "perhaps" in your heart? If He has, what is it? If not, do you want one?

CHAPTER 5

ONE THING IS SURE

*God uses broken things. It takes broken soil to produce
a crop, broken clouds to give rain, broken grain to give
bread, broken bread to give strength. It is the broken
alabaster box that gives forth perfume. It is Peter, weeping
bitterly, who returns to greater power than ever.*

—Vance Havner

Actor Liam Neeson has made four movies titled *Taken*. In the first of the series, his character, Bryan Mills, is a retired CIA agent who adores his seventeen-year-old daughter, Kim. He left the agency to be near her in California, where she lives with her mother and her wealthy stepfather. Kim and her friend Amanda want to travel to Paris, and Kim convinces her mom and stepfather that she'll be fine. Mills isn't so sure. In the taxi on the way from Charles de Gaulle Airport to their hotel in Paris, the two girls share the ride with a stranger, and Amanda impulsively tells him they're alone in the city. When the ride is over, the stranger informs a ring of Albanian thugs who are human traffickers. Only a few minutes into the movie, Albanians break into the girls' apartment. They grab Amanda, but Kim runs and hides under a bed. Frantically, she calls her father. With amazing mental clarity and emotional control in the sudden terror, he tells Kim, "They will take you." He didn't say, "Everything will be fine. Don't worry about it," and he didn't say, "The world is coming to an end!" He gave his daughter the realistic expectation that she couldn't avoid being kidnapped. It was a hard but necessary truth.

What does this scene have to do with leading through chaos? A lot! As leaders, we're in the same place as Bryan Mills. It's up to us to communicate realistic expectations, so our people aren't surprised. Is it possible that rugged realism may be discouraging? That depends. One of the strains of thought—ways of thinking—in some church circles is triumphalism, the belief that God will enable us to go from glory to glory in our daily lives. He will fix every problem and provide every resource. It sounds great, doesn't it? But it flies in the face of Scripture and puts too many of the promises of God in the *already* category instead of the *not yet*. Certainly, God has given us "precious and magnificent promises," but some apply to the Day when all wrongs will be made right, and all sad things will become untrue—in the new heavens and new earth.

We get a much more realistic view of the Christian life by peeling off the lenses that prevent us from seeing the hard realities that are plainly there. Jesus often summoned the people around Him (and us), "Follow Me." Where did His path lead? To misunderstanding, resistance, ridicule, betrayal, torture, and death. If we follow Him, we can expect at least a measure of heartache and pushback. When our expectations are unrealistic, we can't respond well to the hardships when they come. Yes, "They will take you." At different points in our leadership, we'll be attacked, we'll suffer, and we'll feel alone.

WHEN our expectations are unrealistic, we can't respond well to the hardships when they come.

We love to read the first part of Hebrews 11 about God working miracles for people like Enoch, Noah, and Abraham, but notice that it took the intervention of God to rescue them from serious trouble! And even then, they didn't experience the ultimate triumph of perfect peace. The writer tells us,

All these people were still living by faith when they died. They did not receive the things promised; they only saw them and welcomed them from a distance, admitting that they were foreigners and strangers on earth. People who say such things show that they are looking for a country of their own. If they had been thinking of the country they had left, they would have had opportunity to return. Instead, they were longing for a better country—a heavenly one. Therefore God is not ashamed to be called their God, for he has prepared a city for them. —Hebrews 11:13-16

The writer then launches into another list of miraculous interventions in the lives of Abraham (again), Isaac, Jacob, Joseph, and Moses. The stories, it seems, are almost endless because the writer says,

And what more shall I say? I do not have time to tell about Gideon, Barak, Samson and Jephthah, about David and Samuel and the prophets, who through faith conquered kingdoms, administered justice, and gained what was promised; who shut the mouths of lions, quenched the fury of the flames, and escaped the edge of the sword; whose weakness was turned to strength; and who became powerful in battle and routed foreign armies. Women received back their dead, raised to life again. —vv. 32-35a

When we read this, we want to shout, "That's what I'm talking about! Count me in!" But the writer isn't finished:

> There were others who were tortured, refusing to be released so that they might gain an even better resurrection. Some faced jeers and flogging, and even chains and imprisonment. They were put to death by stoning; they were sawed in two; they were killed by the sword. They went about in sheepskins and goatskins, destitute, persecuted and mistreated—the world was not worthy of them. They wandered in deserts and mountains, living in caves and in holes in the ground.
>
> These were all commended for their faith, yet none of them received what had been promised, since God had planned something better for us so that only together with us would they be made perfect. —vv. 35b-40

In fact, God seems to work most powerfully during times of difficulty, and God's purposes are advanced when His people suffer—supremely in Jesus but also when believers stand strong in God's grace through adversity and opposition. The church father Tertullian put it succinctly, "The blood of the martyrs is the seed of the church."[20] This was written in the second century during severe persecution by the Roman authorities.

Jesus promised peace, but it's the peace *in the middle of* difficulties, not an escape from them (John 14:27), and He warned those who followed Him,

> "I tell you, my friends, do not be afraid of those who kill the body and after that can do no more. But I will show you whom you should fear: Fear him who, after your body has been killed, has authority to throw you into hell. Yes, I tell you, fear him. Are not five sparrows sold for two pennies?

---

20 Tertullian, *Apologeticus*, L. 13.

Yet not one of them is forgotten by God. Indeed, the very hairs of your head are all numbered. Don't be afraid; you are worth more than many sparrows. . . .

When you are brought before synagogues, rulers and authorities, do not worry about how you will defend yourselves or what you will say, for the Holy Spirit will teach you at that time what you should say." —Luke 12:4-7, 11-12

If opposition came only from outside the church, it would be easier to handle. It hurts worse when those we trust turn on us. David complained, "Even my close friend, someone I trusted, one who shared my bread, has turned against me" (Psalm 41:9). And Jesus used the same passage in reference to Judas's betrayal, but without the phrase, "someone I trusted" (John 13:18).

So, don't be surprised when you experience chaos. "You will be taken."

SO, DON'T be surprised when you
experience chaos. "You will be taken."

PREDICTABLE SEASONS

As I've consulted with Pastors over several decades, I've noticed patterns of chaos. The most common—and the most significant—include:

Succession and transition of the Pastor

Succession and transition in leadership are just as much about loss as gain. Trust and affection that have been built over many years give way to uncertainty and anxiety. People on the Leadership Team naturally wonder how much their roles (and lives) will be shaken up, and influencers throughout the church probably have a "wait and see" attitude toward the new leader. The exiting Pastor can smooth the runway by preparing people for the change, but even then, a measure of disruption is inevitable. As part of Expand Consulting Partners, I wrote a book to help churches navigate the often turbulent waters of succession and transition. Let me include some observations from this book:

> *Transition occurs by design or default. Unfortunately, we have observed that at least ninety percent of Pastoral transitions occur by default. There is no plan in place to accommodate succession or transition. A Pastor announces retirement, passes away, experiences a moral failure or catastrophic event, and the Board then scrambles to find a replacement, with the urgency of time, not the fit of the candidate, being the major factor in recruitment. Little thought is given to this process ahead of time, although it is of crucial impact to the stagnation or growth of the church. In fact, very few bylaws address succession and transition in any meaningful way.*
>
> *A predetermined plan happens only if the following factors are present.*
>
> 1) *A future-oriented Pastor*
> 2) *A future-oriented church Board*
> 3) *A church that is not personality-driven*
> 4) *A healthy organizational culture*
> 5) *Intentional budgeting for the future*
> 6) *Honor for the present Pastor*

In the same way that a larger plane requires a larger runway, the larger the church, the longer the process of securing the next Pastor. Because of the lack of imminence, resignations or catastrophic events, this stretched timeline allows the Pastor and the church to create a plan non-defensively and inclusively. The best time to talk about something is when there is nothing to defend. The Pastor is loved. The church is viable. The team is functioning. The Lord is blessing. It is in that moment of "non-neediness" that healthy conversations leading to a predetermined plan can save the church from unnecessary damage and harm.

"Life is pleasant. Death is peaceful," wrote the novelist Isaac Asimov. "It's the transition that's troublesome." The same might be said of succession planning. There are only two ways to avoid trouble: be in denial, or be finished with the task. If you're not in one of those places, you're trying to figure out the next step. It is overwhelming, especially if the task is urgent. We urge you to not make haste, but to make adequate preparation.[21]

Major changes on the Leadership Team

Significant personnel changes usually have ripple effects far beyond the Leadership Team. Those who are leaving may have supporters who are upset and assume their friend and mentor was forced out. They may believe the team member wasn't given enough authority or compensation and was treated unfairly. (Of course, if the person was fired, the supporters may feel even more loyal and protective.)

---

21 Samuel R. Chand and Scott Wilson, *Tsunami: Open Secrets to Pastoral Succession & Transition* (Kudu Publishing, 2022), 18, 32, 85.

If the replacement is promoted from within, some level of trust is already present, but those who didn't get tapped for the promotion may be jealous and resentful. If the new person comes from outside, he or she will have to find a way to mesh with the culture of the team, build trust, and become an ally. If the change is in youth ministry, the one leaving may have been highly relational, but the new hire is more transactional . . . or the other way around. A new worship leader may have a different style, or at least a different way of relating to the others on the worship team. The departing executive Pastor may have delegated authority, but a new one may be far more hands-on and high-control. Adjustments will be necessary in every case. It's never as "smooth as glass."

ADJUSTMENTS will be necessary with every personnel change. It's never as "smooth as glass."

Building campaigns

Major building campaigns aren't really about money, bricks, and steel; they're about the people's vision of the future. I've heard more horror stories about building campaigns than I want to remember. In many of these cases, the Pastor moved too quickly, failing to tell stories to prepare the Board, the influencers, and the people so that their excitement virtually demanded the bold new venture. However, most Pastors don't have a lot of experience in real estate and construction, so they need to depend on experts to give sound advice about timing, financing, architecture, and building.

In most churches, stress rises exponentially during these campaigns. The Pastor lives on a knife-edge, wondering, hoping, and praying things will come together, so he won't fall flat on his face. Tension on the team escalates as people add more responsibilities to what they were already doing. Relationships can become frayed, trust eroded or shattered, and the grand vision can turn into a catastrophe... even after the facility is completed.

My recommendation to Pastors is to celebrate the growth they're seeing, but instead of jumping ahead to launch a building campaign, find other ways to capitalize on the growth: add a service, broadcast the services online, expand to multisite campuses, and create new programs and environments in the space they already have. When these (and many other) options have been exhausted, and a larger building is absolutely necessary, it's time to start planning.

Financial challenges

Pastors depend on their Boards to be the financial backbone of the church. Many ask their Boards to tithe and, additionally, to give even more generously to missions and special projects. If Board members are primarily from moderate incomes, this may be problematic, but if only rich people are selected for the Board, that, too, can create difficulties in the expectations of the Board and suspicion among the people.

Everything has a price tag: a new service, a new site, a new program, new technology, more team members, roof repairs

... the list is endless. Without a vision, the people perish, and without money, there's no vision.

Reorganization

I realize *reorganization* is a word that frightens a lot of Pastors and their teams, but reorganization needs arise regularly. Most leaders only make changes in leadership positions and responsibilities when they see a glaring gap, a need that cries out to be met. I have a different strategy: I tell Pastors to ask three questions in the first week of every November:

Whom should I *release*?

Whom should I *retain*?

And whom should I *reassign* (with retraining)?

They need to start talking about these questions with the team in January, so they know the evaluation is coming, then conduct detailed reviews in June, so people on the team have time to shore up any deficiencies before November. Why early November to reorganize? Because you can release people before the holidays and pay them through the end of the year.

To put this into a script, Pastors should tell their teams in January, "I'm going to start something next November that I think will help our team be more effective. In the first week of November, I'm going to ask three questions: Whom should I release? Whom should I retain? And whom should I reassign? I'll make decisions based on my assessments at that time. I want you to know that's coming, and I, or someone I designate, will meet with each of you in June for a performance review. This will give you time to make any course-corrections before November. Any questions?"

Organizations are organisms; that is, they aren't static. People change, situations change, and plans change. It shouldn't be surprising that a leader and the team need a mechanism to promote analysis and restructuring on a regular basis.

Put it on your calendar, and make it happen. If you're reluctant to make hard decisions about people on your team, I completely understand. It's pleasant to give someone a promotion, but it can be excruciating to fire someone you love and trust or reassign someone whose talents no longer meet growing responsibilities.

If you have a lot of people on your Leadership Team, you'll need each department Pastor to ask these questions and make these decisions. If you have no one on your team, but you have volunteers in your smaller church, you can ask the same questions and make similar decisions, but you'll probably do a lot more reassigning than releasing. However, if a volunteer isn't doing the job and doesn't show signs of progress, and that's coupled with a sour disposition, it's time to have some heart-to-heart conversations about what it means to walk with Jesus as a glad and determined servant.

If you follow this advice, regular reorganization will soon become part of the leadership culture of the church. People may be offended or afraid the first time they experience it, but after that, the assessment becomes normal. Far too many Pastors turn a blind eye to people who are in the wrong roles or shouldn't be in a role at all. Do people notice? Of course they do, and the inaction erodes trust in the leader. If the Pastor genuinely doesn't see the problem, that's concerning. If he sees it and doesn't have the courage to do anything about it, that's an even bigger integrity issue.

Most professional plumbers, electricians, attorneys, beauticians, and others have to be recertified each year. How much more should those who work in the kingdom of our Lord and get paid through people's gifts to the church be held to a high standard of excellence? Far too often, we look the other way when someone isn't doing their job well. Oh, we may complain privately, but we can always find reasons to avoid making waves. No one wants to hurt anyone's feelings or bruise someone unnecessarily, but good leadership always involves making tough decisions and having hard conversations. We build trust when people see us treat others with honesty, kindness, and wisdom.

NO ONE wants to hurt anyone's feelings or bruise someone unnecessarily, but good leadership always involves making tough decisions and having hard conversations.

In my book *Who's Holding Your Ladder*, I comment that it's better to have a vacancy on an organizational chart than have the wrong person in the job. If we hang on to people we should have released, we create a multitude of problems for ourselves, the people on our teams, and the people they lead.

Growth

We're thrilled to see new people coming and more lives changed, but growth always creates chaos. Where do we put them? What do they need? What do they expect? How can we connect with them? How can they move from guests to attendees to members to volunteers? Do we have enough space for their children? Where will we find more volunteers to care for their kids?

Some people come with more enthusiasm, vision, and drive than some of the people who were already in the church (and maybe in leadership positions). They bring a different vocabulary which may cause considerable confusion. People who have been comfortable in their roles may feel threatened when new people are recognized and moved into positions of leadership.

Leaders long for and work hard for growth to happen, but it always makes leading more complicated.

Decline

It doesn't take many people leaving to cause considerable consternation in the lives of the Pastor, the Board, the team, and the people who notice their friends aren't sitting next to them in church any longer. The moment they leave isn't the only crucial moment because many conversations have happened *before* that day, and many more happen *after* they're gone. The problem isn't just numbers; it's credibility. When people leave their friends, those left behind naturally wonder if they should leave too. Social media hasn't been kind to Pastors. Snarky online comments aren't part of a recipe for radical commitment and dynamic growth!

Plateaus

Many leaders assume that a plateau—neither growth nor decline—is a terrible place to be, but quite often, it's just a moment of quiet before the next season of growth. Stairs have landings between floors to give us a place to stop and rest, or at least to change direction as we keep moving. These landings aren't optional; they're in the building code.

As the saying goes, an organization that shoots up like a rocket often falls like a rock. Plateaus give leaders the opportunity to consolidate gains, train leaders, and prepare for the next season of growth. (On the Sigmoid Curve, the new vision is implemented at the earliest hints of a plateau.)

To be sure, I've never talked to a Pastor who said, "Sam, I'm planning for a plateau." It has never happened, and it probably never will. But the fact that leaders don't plan for plateaus doesn't mean they won't experience them. They need different muscles to lead in seasons of growth, decline, and plateau—and they can be sure they'll go through all three at different times.

When the church is growing, they need to build a bigger funnel to welcome people at the front end and shepherd them into the life of the church. Just showing up on Sunday is a good start, but good strategic planning, training leaders, creating multiple connection points, and expanding structures are ways to "close the back door" of the church.

In decline, leaders need a combination of relentless optimism and brutal realism, discovering the causes of the decline and responding with faith instead of blame, plans instead of hopelessness, and a renewed commitment to build (or restore) trust.

In seasons of plateau, leaders need to spend time reflecting on what happened during the time of growth, what factors have caused the growth to wane, and what new vision can propel the next season of growth.

A New Vision

Most Pastors don't appreciate the distance between casting a vision and activating it. Jesus taught about the kingdom of God for over three years. He used dozens of passages from the Old Testament, and He told parables to give people a mental image of the concepts. He didn't hesitate to tell His Leadership Team, the disciples, the same message over and over again. We have four gospels, not one. Couldn't we get the picture from one? Maybe, but God wanted us to have the picture painted in four colors, not monochromatic, with four points of view, instead of a single angle.

WE HAVE four gospels, not one. Couldn't we get the picture from one? Maybe, but God wanted us to have the picture painted in four colors, not monochromatic, with four points of view, instead of a single angle.

I've seen Pastors come back from a conference, a sabbatical, or just a time of prayer and announce a sweeping new strategy for the church. It's not surprising that people have a hard time adjusting so quickly! These Pastors jump from thoughts to actions. I recommend a slower approach to incubating the egg of an idea:

» Spend time thinking, praying, and talking with a mentor, or at most a few close friends, but keep the ideas confidential for a while. This gives time for the ideas to ripen and coalesce.

» When you're ready (and you'll know when that time comes), carefully craft the vision on paper, and ask your mentor or close friends to review it carefully and give you feedback.

» Do your homework to study the history of your church to find compelling stories of faith, courage, and God's provision.

» When you've taken time to fine-tune the vision, introduce it to the person on your Board who is the key player. If that person doesn't buy it, take a step back and regroup.

» Share the vision with the whole Board, and ask the key Board member to communicate his or her enthusiasm for it.

» Share it with your team, and tell them no question is off the table. Answer every question with respect and thoroughness, but realize you'll have to often say, "I don't know, but we'll find out."

» Meet with influencers to inform them and get their feedback.

» Ask people in responsible positions on the Board and the team to meet with you to hammer out the implementation process in detail.

» Carefully plan the rollout to the rest of the leaders in the church, the congregation, and, if appropriate, the community.

» Then and only then are the plans implemented, and again, with care, patience, and wisdom. And even then, keep teaching the concepts, keep encouraging people, and keep painting the picture of the vision fulfilled.

Don't be in a hurry. When we look at stories in the Scriptures, we see long periods between the vision cast and the vision activated. Abraham had to wait twenty-five years for the promise of a son to be fulfilled. Scholars suggest David had to wait twenty-five years after Samuel anointed him until he was crowned king. Nehemiah built the walls of Jerusalem in only fifty-two days, but we need to remember that he had been the cupbearer to the king in Susa, the capital of Persia. In that role, he was both the most trusted and the least dispensable servant.

It undoubtedly took many years for Nehemiah to rise to that trusted position in the king's presence. He tasted everything that was given to the king. If anything was poisoned, he was the first to go. When he heard the plight of the people in Jerusalem, he was grieved, and he summoned the courage to ask the king for permission to build the walls. He was granted favor to secure the resources, and after traveling hundreds of miles to get lumber from the forest and take it to Jerusalem, he met with the people of the city to enlist them in the work. From that point, he expertly managed the rebuilding process even though he experienced fierce opposition. After Jesus met Saul of Tarsus on the road to Damascus, Saul, now Paul, spent three years in Arabia and then about ten years in Tarsus pouring through the Scriptures to craft his message.

It's wonderful that God speaks to us at conferences (that's why we go!), through books, on sabbaticals, through podcasts, and in conversations with those we respect, but the seed isn't the fruit... at least, not yet. The Bible uses agrarian metaphors to remind us that the seed has potential, but it's only unlocked through time and the right conditions. When we rush the process, we short-circuit God's pattern.

SEED HAS potential, but it's only unlocked through time and the right conditions. When we rush the process, we short-circuit God's pattern.

LITTLE BY LITTLE

Exodus is the supreme narrative of the Jewish people, and it's the prologue of the bigger story of Jesus bringing us out of slavery to sin and death and into His kingdom. The twelve spies came back with a doubt-filled majority report and a faith-filled minority report. God's people then spent forty years traveling a distance that could have been accomplished in a couple of weeks. Along the way, God gave them plenty of warnings and instructions. A passage that has meant a lot to me is both a warning and a promise. God, again, promised that He would drive out the Hivites, Canaanites, and Hittites from the land:

"But I will not drive them out in a single year, because the land would become desolate and the wild animals too numerous for you. Little by little I will drive them out before you, until you have increased enough to take possession of the land." —Exodus 23:29-30

For me, this is the most encouraging leadership passage in the Bible. Let me explain.

God is all-powerful. He can accomplish any task instantly with the snap of His fingers, but He has chosen to operate through processes. A common theme in the Bible is "waiting on the Lord." This isn't just about time; it's about attitude. As we wait, God prepares us, He prepares others, and He prepares situations. If we truly believe He's at work behind the scenes when we can't see His hand, we'll wait patiently and productively. "Little by little." That's the pattern of change and growth in the Bible. Jesus used metaphors of soil and seeds to remind us that God's work is progressive. God explained that He didn't drive out the people of the land too quickly because His people couldn't handle it. I'm convinced that the growth of churches isn't always explosive and dynamic, "up and to the right," because we can't handle it either. We would become cocky or complacent . . . or maybe both, instead of being dependent on God to do what only He can do in His timing and His way.

The ability to handle surprises is directly related to the clarity of expectations. If my birthday is coming and I've caught wind that Brenda and the girls have planned a party for me, when I open the door and they yell, "Surprise!" it's very pleasant, but it's not surprising. If, though, I had no clue they were planning a party, and I walked through the door,

I'd be very surprised. Our job as Pastors is to give hints that something is coming. No, it's much more than hints—we need to give people plenty of information and compelling stories to prepare them for the next season in the life of the church. It's almost impossible to over-communicate, so whatever you think is enough, it probably isn't.

By nature, most Pastors are optimistic and trusting, and they see potential in everyone they meet. These positive traits, though, may not equip them to share new ideas. They expect people to understand quickly and jump on the train, so they're shocked when they experience hesitance and, more than that, genuine opposition. But that kind of chaos is avoidable. They need to understand that the gap between sharing the vision and implementing it needs to be filled with gripping narratives and inspiring teaching—not just for the congregation but for the Board and the team, too.

My simple questions are:

» What are you doing to bring your people along? (Are you teaching them the alphabet and basic grammar before you expect them to read Shakespeare?)

» What are you doing to reset their expectations, so they're more realistic?

» What are you doing to reset your own?

The questions may be simple, but answering them is absolutely necessary. As we craft our message to take people through stages of growth "little by little," we can reflect on another passage of Scripture about a process. In the last chapters of Ezekiel, the prophet is accompanied by a guide on a "temple tour." Going through the inner courts and the outer ones, Ezekiel sees the kitchens equipped to cook the sacrifices. Then the guide takes him to the door of the sanctuary where he sees water flowing near the altar. The guide led him to the north gate, the one that faced east, and the water is ankle-deep. More water flows, and Ezekiel is now knee-deep. Then the vision shows the flow of more water, and he is waist-deep. Finally, the prophet is in over his head, and he has to swim. When he gets back to the bank, the guide explains the meaning of the vision:

> "This water flows toward the eastern region and goes down into the Arabah, where it enters the Dead Sea. When it empties into the sea, the salty water there becomes fresh. Swarms of living creatures will live wherever the river flows. There will be large numbers of fish, because this water flows there and makes the salt water fresh; so where the river flows everything will live.... Fruit trees of all kinds will grow on both banks of the river. Their leaves will not wither, nor will their fruit fail. Every month they will bear fruit, because the water from the sanctuary flows to them. Their fruit will serve for food and their leaves for healing."
> —Ezekiel 47:8-9, 12

You and I are being led by our guide, the Holy Spirit. He doesn't plunge us into water that's over our heads at the beginning. He gives us time to get acclimated to the levels of clarity and intensity. If we're patient and stay in the water, amazing things can happen. The transformation of the water and land in the vision was a picture of the transformation of people and nations, a process that will be ultimately fulfilled in the New Jerusalem of Revelation 22.

> GOD LEADS us through seasons in our churches—seasons that have their own inherent chaos. Our task is to reframe these changing times with a lot of teaching and stories as we expect the stages to play out over time.

In the meantime, God leads us through seasons in our churches—seasons that have their own inherent chaos. Our task is to reframe these changing times with a lot of teaching and stories as we expect the stages to play out over time. Our realistic expectations and commitment to the process will help our people, those entrusted to us by God, make the most of every season we experience together. But remember, one thing is certain: "You will be taken."

We want to avoid suffering, death, sin, ashes. But we live in a world crushed and broken and torn, a world God Himself visited to redeem. We receive his poured-out life, and being allowed the high privilege of suffering with Him, may then pour ourselves out for others.
—Elisabeth Elliot

CONSIDER THIS:

1) Who is someone you know who is both ruthlessly realistic and relentlessly hopeful? What is this person's impact on you and others?

2) What are some outcomes when people are surprised by their problems? How would it have helped to anticipate them?

3) Which of the seasons described in this chapter are you facing now? What principles do you need to focus on to maximize this time?

4) We live in an instant society, with instant banking, microwave cooking, and the entire world of information available with a few keystrokes. How do you think modern life has affected our ability to be patient and persistent in seeing a vision implemented and fulfilled?

5) Let me ask you: What are you doing to bring your people along?

6) What are you doing to reset their expectations, so they're more realistic?

7) What are you doing to reset your own?

CHAPTER 6

PASTORING THE PUSHBACK

The authority by which the Christian leader leads is not power but love, not force but example, not coercion but reasoned persuasion. Leaders have power, but power is safe only in the hands of those who humble themselves to serve.

—John Stott

S uspicion about our motives, criticism before they understand, and juicy gossip about only part of the information ... these are just a few ways Pastors experience pushback when they share a new, big vision. To be sure, those who trust the Pastor almost always give the benefit of the doubt, so we can surmise that the level of doubt among Board and team members is directly correlated to the level of distrust.

I've seen dozens of instances when Pastors felt blindsided by criticism. For instance:

» A Pastor promoted a youth Pastor to the executive team and put him in charge of discipleship, but several others believed they were more qualified.

» Another Pastor looked outside his team to hire an executive Pastor, someone who had no experience with the culture but had the skills the church desperately needed. Some people on the Leadership Team saw only the culture clash, not the needed talents.

» When the concept of multisite churches was relatively new, a Pastor communicated the idea as a solution to the limitations of their current facilities. It made perfect sense to him, but a few Board members had no clue something like this could work.

» When a youth ministry exploded in size, the Pastor repurposed a wing of the church to accommodate the bigger crowds. The team members who had been officing there resented being asked to move.

Starting new programs virtually always necessitates adjustments in responsibilities. Some may feel honored, some may feel overlooked, and some may feel burdened by the weight of added, seemingly thankless tasks. In the vast majority of these (and many other) instances, the Pastor didn't communicate early enough, frequently enough, or fully enough.

I've been asked to work with Pastors and their teams when there has been a significant disconnect over a new vision. On one occasion, the Pastor felt it was his responsibility to be nothing but positive. When he shared the vision, he always painted it in glowing terms, and it seemed to people on his team that he had no idea what disruptions it would create for them. When they asked questions about the process to clarify their roles, he seemed offended and gave quick, simplistic answers . . . which only eroded trust even more.

Some Pastors, like that one, misinterpret questions from their Board and Leadership Team. I've noticed that when Boomer Pastors hear the question "Why?" they often see it as a personal challenge to their authority and a statement of dishonor, but Millennials, Gen Xers, and Gen Zers have grown up asking why about virtually everything. To them, it's natural, normal, and right. Boomer Pastors often react with a condescending attitude instead of giving a thoughtful answer.

BENEFITS OF ANTICIPATION

It's important for Pastors to expect pushback and welcome it. If they don't expect it, they'll probably be surprised and reactionary. Anticipating hard questions gives us time to prepare, to gather more information, and to avoid reverse pushback, which occurs when the Pastor feels threatened and growls something like, "Are you for me or against me?" That never turns out well.

> **ANTICIPATING** hard questions gives us time to prepare, to gather more information, and to avoid reverse pushback, which occurs when the Pastor feels threatened and growls something like, "Are you for me or against me?" That never turns out well.

Pastors instinctively know who will jump on board pretty quickly, who will need a little time to process the information, and who will ask hard questions—and keep asking more of them after the first ones are answered. Sometimes Pastors are confused when they share a new idea, and they get some opposition or at least some reluctance to embrace it. They hear the "Amens" when they preach, but they can't expect instant "Amens" from the members of the Board and the Leadership Team when they roll out a grand plan. The anointing in the pulpit doesn't follow them into the office. They are two very different environments, requiring two different modes of communication, with two different sets of expectations.

If we anticipate good questions, we'll be ready. Inevitably, someone who has heard the presentation asks, "But Pastor, what about...?" Imagine the difference if the Pastor responds, "That's a great question. Here's the way I see it right now, but I want your input along the way," or "How dare you! You just need to trust me!" Honest questions are very different from genuine opposition, and the two shouldn't be confused or equated.

I've seen four distinct types of responses from team and Board members:

» Open opposition, which occurs when relationships are already strained.

» Behind-the-scenes alliances, which thrive on gossip and innuendo.

» Disengagement, which occurs as people give up on any hope of being understood and valued.

» Honest inquiry, which is the kind of participation that's based on trust and actually deepens trust between the Pastor and the others.

Without investing in open, honest, trusting relationships, leaders are asking for trouble when they communicate big changes are coming. But when trust has been established, honest questions are a sign of strength and health, not opposition. Of course, it's certainly possible that some people trust the Pastor and others don't—in fact, it may be just one, and this may be one of the most important teachable moments for that one.

WITHOUT investing in open, honest, trusting relationships, leaders are asking for trouble when they communicate big changes are coming.

OUR EXAMPLE

One of the most famous interchanges in the gospels is when Nicodemus came to Jesus at night. He may have come after dark because he was afraid of other Pharisees seeing him with Jesus, but whatever his underlying motive, the point is that he took the initiative to come. He started with an affirming statement:

> *"Rabbi, we know that you are a teacher who has come from God. For no one could perform the signs you are doing if God were not with him." —John 3:2*

In response, Jesus took Nicodemus beyond the observation of His ministry to expose the longing of his heart: "Very truly I tell you, no one can see the kingdom of God unless they are born again" (v. 3).

Nicodemus didn't react by exclaiming, "You're nuts!" or "You make no sense at all!" Instead, he asked for more information. "How can someone be born when they are old? Surely they cannot enter a second time into their mother's womb and be born!" (v. 4)

Jesus wasn't offended in the least. He didn't ridicule Nicodemus for asking a dumb question, and He didn't throw up His hands and walk away. He took the opportunity to explain more about the Spirit and the kingdom of God:

> *"Very truly I tell you, no one can enter the kingdom of God unless they are born of water and the Spirit. Flesh gives birth to flesh, but the Spirit gives birth to spirit. You should not be surprised at my saying, 'You must be born again.' The wind blows wherever it pleases. You hear its sound, but you cannot tell where it comes from or where it is going. So it is with everyone born of the Spirit." (vv. 5-8)*

Again, Nicodemus expressed his incredulity—he simply didn't understand what Jesus was saying. "How can this be?" Jesus patiently continued His explanation, gently prodding Nicodemus to consider that his role as a leader included the responsibility to communicate these things to others:

"You are Israel's teacher," said Jesus, "and do you not understand these things? Very truly I tell you, we speak of what we know, and we testify to what we have seen, but still you people do not accept our testimony. I have spoken to you of earthly things and you do not believe; how then will you believe if I speak of heavenly things? No one has ever gone into heaven except the one who came from heaven—the Son of Man. Just as Moses lifted up the snake in the wilderness, so the Son of Man must be lifted up, that everyone who believes may have eternal life in him." (vv. 10-15)

But Jesus wasn't finished. He shifted from the Old Testament analogy of Moses lifting up the snake, so those who looked were saved, to the future when Jesus would be lifted up and those who look to Him are saved:

"For God so loved the world that he gave his one and only Son, that whoever believes in him shall not perish but have eternal life. For God did not send his Son into the world to condemn the world, but to save the world through him. Whoever believes in him is not condemned, but whoever does not believe stands condemned already because they have not believed in the name of God's one and only Son. This is the verdict: Light has come into the world, but people loved darkness instead of light because their deeds were evil. Everyone who does evil hates the light, and will not come into the light for fear that their deeds will be exposed.

But whoever lives by the truth comes into the light, so that
it may be seen plainly that what they have done has been
done in the sight of God." —John 3:16-21

We usually look at this passage as an important gospel message, and it's certainly that, but we can also view it as the Master's class on how to handle questions.

Sadly, there are too few interchanges like this with the Pharisees and Sadducees. More often, their questions were designed to trip up Jesus, to make Him look like a fool . . . or a rebel . . . or both. For instance, they demanded to see a sign from Him (Matthew 12:38-42 and 16:1-4), and they plotted with the hated Herodians (who were allied with the Roman occupiers) to force Jesus to declare if He would pay taxes— and show that He was complicit with the Romans—or not pay them—and prove that He was leading a separatist movement as a rebel (Mark 12:13-17). They asked which is the greatest commandment, hoping He would stumble, and they could condemn Him (Matthew 22:34-36), they brought a woman caught in adultery to see if He would follow the law and order her to be stoned (John 8:3-4), and, on several occasions, they reviled Jesus for healing people on the Sabbath (Matthew 12:9-14, et al.).

Perhaps the climax of the fierce confrontations was recorded by John. Jesus had fed the five thousand, and the people followed Him because they wanted more food. He tried to explain that He was offering far more than loaves of bread, but they didn't want to hear His gracious offer of spiritual food. The argument rose in intensity until Jesus had had enough. He told them, "I am the bread of life. Whoever comes to me will never go hungry, and whoever believes in me will never be thirsty. But as I told you, you have seen me and still you do not believe." They continued to complain that He wouldn't miraculously feed them again, so He tried to point them to something far more nourishing than the physical bread He had given them:

> "I am the bread of life. Your ancestors ate the manna in the wilderness, yet they died. But here is the bread that comes down from heaven, which anyone may eat and not die. I am the living bread that came down from heaven. Whoever eats this bread will live forever. This bread is my flesh, which I will give for the life of the world."

Again they complained, so He said something that was unimaginable to them:

> "Very truly I tell you, unless you eat the flesh of the Son of Man and drink his blood, you have no life in you. Whoever eats my flesh and drinks my blood has eternal life, and I will raise them up at the last day. For my flesh is real food and my blood is real drink. Whoever eats my flesh and drinks my blood remains in me, and I in them. Just as the living Father sent me and I live because of the Father, so the one who feeds on me will live because of me. This is the bread that came down from heaven. Your ancestors ate manna and died, but whoever feeds on this bread will live forever."
> —John 6:35-40, 48-51, 53-58

Is this an example of how we should handle opposition? Yes, sometimes it is but only after we've tried again and again to love, explain, demonstrate, and love even more. Two verses in the Proverbs seem to be contradictory, but they're a source of insight into how to handle difficult people:

> Do not answer a fool according to his folly,

or you yourself will be just like him.
Answer a fool according to his folly,
or he will be wise in his own eyes. —Proverbs 26:4-5

I believe this is saying to answer a difficult person once, twice, and maybe another time or two, but there comes a point when we lose ourselves (and our point) in the confrontation, and we're just as foolish as the other person if we continue. Thankfully, that's seldom the case with our Leadership Teams and Boards, but it happens. Believe me, it happens.

I often tell Pastors, "You can pastor a church with only one spiritual gift, but you desperately need that one: it's the gift of discernment. With it, you can navigate any storms; without it, you're sunk." When we review the life of Jesus, we see this trait in glaring lights. He responded to each person and each situation with perfect wisdom. He was amazingly kind and gentle with the wayward and the sick, He was amazingly patient with those who followed Him, and He was amazingly shrewd in His conversations with those who opposed Him.

I OFTEN tell Pastors, "You can pastor a church with only one spiritual gift, but you desperately need that one: it's the gift of discernment.

Discernment gives insight about the question behind the question. Someone may turn up his nose at an idea and ask "Why?" but you can tell if this is really an honest, searching question…or a challenge to your authority. When in doubt, assume it's honest. You'll find out soon enough whether it is or not!

I've observed some Pastors who have lacked the gift of discernment and totally overreacted to honest questions. I've seen a Pastor resign on the spot, I've seen a Pastor throw a chair across the room, and I heard another one curse at his team. But I've also seen more than one Pastor step into the moment and say, "I sense a lot of tension in the room, and I don't think we're communicating in a way that pleases God. Let's take a recess to recalibrate our hearts and minds. We'll pray for wisdom and pick it up again in our next meeting." I've also seen a Pastor respond to pushback by saying, "I see what you're saying, and you're making some good points. I need to go back and think about this before we continue our discussion. When I came in today, I was very sure of my position, but you've raised issues I hadn't considered. The idea will be better because of your input. God has put you in my life for many reasons, and this is one of them. You've given me the opportunity to be a wiser person and a better leader. Thank you."

Actually, every Pastor I've ever known has felt like reacting harshly at one point or another. A high level of frustration comes with the job, and from time to time, they've considered the benefits of giving up and walking away. But the vast majority have responded more often like the last example—they've been patient and kind. (The Pastors who claim they've never wanted to quit are either lying or cut from a different bolt of cloth than the rest of us!)

IN THEIR SHOES

Some of the Pastors reading this book have only recently been called to that role, and they remember very well what it was like to be on a Leadership Team. Others, however, have been in the role long enough to forget. To develop the twin traits of patience and persistence, we need to put ourselves in the shoes of those we lead.

» They don't see what the leader sees, and in fact, they *can't* see what the leader sees. That's not a flaw in them. It's simply the reason the Pastor is the leader. Those team members who develop the capacity to see farther and more clearly are primed to take a larger role, perhaps in another church.

» They have limited responsibility, but the Pastor carries the burden of it all. I often tell Pastors, "You're the only one in your church who goes to sleep every night and gets up every morning thinking about the church." Everyone else can take a vacation and put their church involvement on ice for a week or two, but the Pastor can't. Even on vacation at the beach, fishing in a mountain stream, or on a Mediterranean cruise, concerns for the church continue . . . all day, every day. Doctors, attorneys, engineers, teachers, and plumbers can turn off the mental switches for a while, but Pastors can't and don't. If something tragic happens and television cameras show up on the front lawn, they're looking for the Pastor—and no one else. Banks get nervous when leadership at a church changes because they aren't sure what to expect from the new Pastor. That's why they insist on a succession plan before they make a loan. They know the senior Pastor is the person whose heart is in the church, and they're counting on that person to fulfill the obligations.

» **They haven't yet developed the capacity to lead the whole church.** They're focused on their sphere of responsibility, not the entire church. That's completely good, right, and expected. However, if a Pastor notices that one of the team members is growing in capacity, it may be time to affirm it and release that person to a larger role, either at that church or another one. On the other hand, two specific roles have a limited shelf life: No one has an eighty-year-old worship leader, and youth Pastors usually move on to other roles when they're too old to keep up with the kids. Many of them become senior Pastors. This means that every year, youth Pastors are farther down the runway to their next role. If Pastors don't understand that reality, they won't prepare for the transition and be ready for the new hire.

» **They view change as a threat to their identity on the team.** This usually happens when the Pastor hasn't affirmed their strengths, gifts, and contributions, leaving team members feeling more vulnerable during times of change. Pastors need to have the voice of a beloved mentor to say often and clearly, "You're doing such a great job. I've seen you grow and develop, and you handled that difficult situation really wisely. I'm really proud of you!" Conversations like this provide a wealth of stability and confidence. Team members need reassurance that the Pastor sees them and appreciates them. It's not a deficiency that they need affirmation— we all need it! Think of how many passages in Scripture affirm our place as God's beloved, treasured children. We need to hear it from God's Word, and we need to hear it from each other. People have done this for me. Many years ago, someone said, "Sam, I can see God using you to lead people." Another said, "I believe you have the gifts and calling to be a Pastor." Later, someone said, "Sam, it seems you have a real talent for helping people thrive in their roles." And somewhere along the way, a friend said, "Those ideas need to be in a book." I don't know where I'd be today if those people, and many more, hadn't seen something in me and called it out of me.

» **They blame the leader for any discomfort and take it as a personal offense.** When people wonder if we're for them, if we value them, if we appreciate their contribution to the team, they're naturally defensive. So let's put it the other way around: If a person is defensive, it may well mean that we haven't done a good job of providing a firm foundation of encouragement. In our communication, we need to notice that team members are very different from each other, so they require a tailored approach from us. For instance, I have two daughters. They share a lot of genes, but their personalities are miles apart. When they were little, if Rachel was doing something wrong and I merely glanced at her, she melted in tears of regret. Debbie, on the other hand, needed a more direct approach.

If you have more than one person on your team, you need to tailor your communication to each one, at least to some extent. You never punish people when they mess up; you always disciple them. Punishment looks back at the wrong, but discipleship points to future growth and usefulness. This distinction matters—it matters a lot.

IF YOU HAVE more than one person on your team, you need to tailor your communication to each one, at least to some extent.

» **They haven't learned to live with a measure of ambiguity.** This is one of the most important lessons we can impart to those on our teams. Insecure leaders have to be right all the time, have all the answers, and never be in doubt. Secure, wise, mature leaders know that they don't know all that much, and they're comfortable saying, "I don't know." When team members are in that environment, they can relax and admit when they don't know all the answers. Together, then, they can look for solutions and realize that virtually every element of ministry involves a process of discovery. One of the statements I'm learning to say is, "I don't know yet. I'm still working through my doubts." In his book *Reaching for the Invisible God*, Philip Yancey quotes Andrew Greeley: "If one wishes to eliminate uncertainty, tension, confusion and disorder from one's life, there is no point in getting mixed up either with Yahweh or with Jesus of Nazareth." Yancey reflects on his own experience, "I grew up expecting that a relationship with God would bring order, certainty, and a calm rationality to life. Instead, I have discovered that living in faith involves much dynamic tension."[22]

I appreciate leaders who are comfortable enough to say, "I have an idea, but I don't know how it might work out," "I need to pray, study, and talk to people about this before we take any steps," "It would be good to do a feasibility study," "Give me some honest feedback about this concept." These leaders know that life and leadership are journeys.

SHEPHERDING YOUR FLOCK

As we pastor the people on our teams, our Boards, and other influencers in our churches, we need to invite questions, affirm people who ask them, and be patient with those who don't catch on very quickly. Everyone is watching to see how we respond. If we show we aren't offended, and we don't treat them like fools or enemies, we'll earn a little more trust from everyone. They expect us to lead, but they hope we'll lead with a blend of boldness and kindness, following the example of the Lion and Lamb.

PEOPLE expect us to lead, but they hope we'll lead with a blend of boldness and kindness, following the example of the Lion and Lamb.

Jesus obviously learned the value of honest questions very early in His life. We only have a brief glimpse of His

22 Philip Yancey, *Reaching for the Invisible God* (Grand Rapids: Zondervan, 2000), 92.

formative years, but it's instructive. Luke takes us to the temple when Jesus was twelve years old. Mary and Joseph thought Jesus was with their group when they left Jerusalem to travel back to Nazareth, but on the road, they discovered He wasn't there!

> When they did not find him, they went back to Jerusalem to look for him. After three days they found him in the temple courts, sitting among the teachers, listening to them and asking them questions. Everyone who heard him was amazed at his understanding and his answers. —Luke 2:45-47 (emphasis added)

He was doing what we're hoping our team members will do when we talk to them: He was listening, asking questions, gaining understanding, and sharing His ideas with others. In personal coaching, we recognize the power of questions to draw people out and stimulate self-discovery. Jesus, even as a young man, knew the power of questions, and He used them effectively throughout His ministry.

But Jesus wasn't afraid to surprise and disappoint His disciples. In one of the most remarkable days recorded in the gospels, Jesus taught in the synagogue, healed Peter's mother-in-law, and then:

> "[healed] all the sick and demon-possessed. The whole town gathered at the door, and Jesus healed many who had various diseases. He also drove out many demons, but he would not let the demons speak because they knew who he was." —Mark 1:32-34

You know how exhausting a full day of ministry can be, but Jesus interrupted His sleep that night to be alone and pray. The next morning, the disciples were ready for a repeat of the glories of the previous day. When they found Him, they exclaimed, "Everyone is looking for you!" No kidding! I would guess the town and the hillsides were full of people wanting to see Jesus. But He had a different agenda: "'Let us go somewhere else—to the nearby villages—so I can preach there also. That is why I have come.' So he traveled throughout Galilee, preaching in their synagogues and driving out demons" (vv. 35-39).

I would have loved to see the look on the faces of Peter and the rest of the disciples. They were sure Jesus should stay. After all, great things were happening! But Jesus' vision was bigger than theirs and different from theirs. They may have been perplexed, but they followed Him. He saw what they couldn't see, He had responsibilities that were far beyond theirs, and He had an unlimited capacity to do the Father's will.

As we lead our people, there will be times when we feel led to take the church somewhere no one else can imagine. If we've built relationships of trust and affirmation, they'll go with us. They may shake their heads for the first mile or two of the trip, but soon, they'll be with us as partners.

The true shepherd spirit is an amalgam of many precious graces. He is hot with zeal, but he is not fiery with passion. He is gentle, and yet he rules his class. He is loving, but he does not wink at sin. He has power over the lambs, but he is not domineering or sharp. He has cheerfulness, but not levity; freedom, but not license; solemnity, but not gloom.
—Charles Spurgeon

CONSIDER THIS:

1) When have you seen a leader handle pushback really well? What did the leader's example do for the team ... and for you?

2) When have you seen pushback handled in a way that eroded or shattered trust? How were you affected?

3) Why is it important for leaders to realize that no one else can see what they see? Why is it important for the team members to understand this truth?

4) No matter what your role may be on the team, you're a leader. What are some ways you can put yourself in the shoes of those on your team?

5) Are you comfortable with ambiguity? Explain your answer.

6) What kind of relationships have to be developed so that the leader's surprising agenda doesn't derail the team?

CHAPTER 7

PREDICTABLE STAGES

*A leader is one who knows the way, goes
the way, and shows the way.*

—John C. Maxwell

As I've observed Pastors and their leadership, I've noticed that many take their churches through stages, actually, thoroughly predictable stages. They often begin as *entrepreneurs*, either launching the church or bringing new ideas and energy to an existing church. Within weeks or months, the shape of the vision *emerges*. After a while, the new concepts, structures, and culture become *established*. However, sooner or later, the Pastor faces a fork in the road: stagnation causes the vision to *erode*, or the Pastor has the insight to launch a new *enterprise* to reinvigorate the team and the church.

Planting a church gives Pastors the opportunity to create the culture during the prelaunch period, but being called to an existing church requires more patience and wisdom to recreate an organizational culture. I've consulted with a man, I'll call him Dave, who, at thirty-one years old, was called to a church that had been in existence for over a century. For decades, a few families had dominated the Board, resisting new ideas, leaving the series of Pastors feeling frustrated and impotent. Dave's youth worked for him and against him— several of the people on the Board were sure he would be putty in their hands, but Dave's enthusiasm to reach beyond the walls of the church captured the hearts of many in the congregation . . . and even some Board members.

PLANTING a church gives Pastors the
opportunity to create the culture during the
prelaunch period, but being called to an existing
church requires more patience and wisdom
to recreate an organizational culture.

No one in leadership argued about the goal of reaching the lost and helping the disadvantaged in the community. The question was how they would invest their resources to do it. When the church began in the early twentieth century, the Pastor and church leaders could expect people in the community to come to them. Back then, the church was seen as a vital part of the life of the community. Now, that's far less true. Dave involved his team and his Board in a process of discovery. They asked, "How can we have an impact for Christ in the lives of people who increasingly see the church as irrelevant?" Together, they crafted a plan, communicated it to the congregation, and launched their efforts.

As the strategy took effect and changes emerged, some people in the church felt excited about making a difference in their neighborhoods, but others complained, "This isn't the way we've done things!" Some families left the church and joined congregations down the street, and other families left without finding a new church home, but many new families and individuals began coming. Some of those who left had been part of the financial backbone of the church for decades, but many of the newcomers had no concept of tithing and sacrificial giving. A few members of the team were uncomfortable with the inevitable changes in the scope of their responsibility. No job description remained untouched, and all the proposed transitions proved to be too much for a few people. So ... a few were released, one retired, two were hired, and everyone else had at least part of their role reassigned and realigned.

To his credit, Dave anticipated all of this, so he wasn't caught off guard as he experienced pushback when the new vision began to emerge in the life of the church.

About nine months into the new strategy, everyone involved could see fresh signs of health and growth. They could accurately predict attendance and seasonal changes in patterns of giving. The worship team had gelled, the gathering of information for announcements had been streamlined, and they had worked hard to recruit enough qualified volunteers for the children's ministry. The auditorium was packed, so they started a second service. Finances had stabilized, and there was an air of excitement throughout the church. Then, two Board members asked to meet with Dave.

They told him that the bylaws and accounting system needed to be updated, so everyone was clear about the church's form and function. (The last time they'd been reviewed in any detail was four decades earlier.) Dave saw the wisdom in their observation, so he tapped them to study the issues and make a recommendation to the Board. They spent several months gathering information and crafting the first draft of new bylaws. The proposed changes prompted rich discussions, and the bylaws were accepted with a few revisions. Better structures and clearer communication were an essential part of the church's development—which is exactly what happens when a vision emerges and becomes established.

Four years into the new initiative, things were humming at Dave's church. The initial hesitation by some was long forgotten. Dave had implemented an effective discipleship program to help the new people grow in their faith, and some of them were already in leadership positions. But Dave's heart felt restless. He and I had talked about the Sigmoid Curve and the need to launch new initiatives before an organization plateaus and declines. Growth had brought the challenges of hard decisions that hadn't been answered: to add yet another service, build a larger facility, launch a multisite strategy, or spin off new churches as core teams were developed.

He spent time talking with me and other Pastors he trusts, and he felt led to launch a new concept to create a church-planting school. Some on the Board were thrilled, but a few wondered why Dave couldn't be happy with all the good things they were doing in the community and all the people who had come to Christ and had become regular attenders and members. Dave's concept would again require the staff team and Board to realign their responsibilities, and at least a couple of them would shift entirely to run the new school. To create a residency program for aspiring church planters, they wanted to enlist the involvement of other churches in the area.

Gradually, the concept began to take shape, and a year later, they launched their residency program with seven men and two women who were dedicated to being bi-vocational during the two-year program and then planting churches wherever God led them. The new director of the program had experience planting a church, and the mentors were Pastors in the area who had started the churches where they served. The director, the mentors, and other leaders from around the area trained the students in classes, workshops, and outreaches.

This effort required Dave and other participating Pastors to raise the money for the program, and it injected new energy into all the churches involved. Gradually, the program expanded to include planting churches overseas, and residency programs were developed in three countries: Argentina, Kenya, and Indonesia.

Dave has been at the church for only twelve years, but in that brief time, God has used him to raise the level of vision, expectations, and involvement at every level of the organization ... and create a few new departments.

Within a few years, Dave's church went through one set of stages and then launched another. It looked something like this:

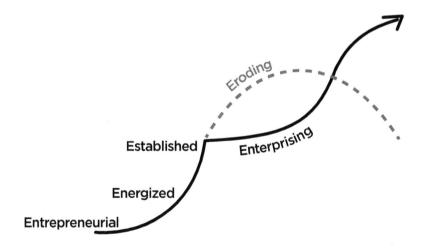

ANTICIPATED LOSSES

One of the traits I learned to appreciate about Dave is that he developed an appetite for loss. From his earliest days as a Pastor, he understood that a bold vision is always a dividing line: people are for it or against it, some will be attracted and some repelled, some will join the church to participate in the new vision, but some will leave. He wasn't surprised when he experienced the full range of responses.

WISE LEADERS wrestle with the hard question of what and whom they're willing to lose for the sake of possible gains.

Wise leaders wrestle with the hard question of what and whom they're willing to lose for the sake of possible gains. This isn't an academic exercise. From the outset of a bold idea, they can imagine adverse reactions from some people who like things just the way they are (and always have been).

The word most often used to describe Jesus' emotions in the gospels is *compassion*, which means to be deeply moved by the plight of another person. Jesus' tender empathy and concern for hurting people were traits that stood out to Matthew, Mark, Luke, and John, but time after time, we see Him moving on after a stunning, miraculous moment. He had His eye on something far bigger than the disciples could see, and nothing could stop Him. In one of the most poignant scenes, we return to the passage where people followed Jesus because they wanted another free lunch, but He offered them the Bread of

Life. They didn't want what He offered, so the crowd, probably numbering in the thousands, turned and walked away. Jesus didn't beg them to stay. In fact, He turned to those closest to Him and asked, "You do not want to leave too, do you?"

I can almost hear the tension in Peter's voice when he answered, "Lord, to whom shall we go? You have the words of eternal life. We have come to believe and to know that you are the Holy One of God" (John 6:66-69). At that moment, Peter had at least a glimpse of the cost of following Jesus.

Paul, too, counted the cost. His first letter to the Corinthians was corrective, like a disappointed father admonishing his child to do better. In the opening comments of his second letter, Paul poured out his heart about the price he had paid to represent Jesus:

> We do not want you to be uninformed, brothers and sisters, about the troubles we experienced in the province of Asia. We were under great pressure, far beyond our ability to endure, so that we despaired of life itself. Indeed, we felt we had received the sentence of death. But this happened that we might not rely on ourselves but on God, who raises the dead. He has delivered us from such a deadly peril, and he will deliver us again. On him we have set our hope that he will continue to deliver us. —2 Corinthians 1:8-10

Paul was convinced he was going to die for his faith. In the same letter, several chapters later, he included a litany of heartaches and hardships he endured to take the gospel of grace to those who had never heard. Some religious leaders had obviously told the Corinthians that they shouldn't pay attention to Paul any longer, and he responded by pointing out a stark contrast:

Are they servants of Christ? (I am out of my mind to talk like this.) I am more. I have worked much harder, been in prison more frequently, been flogged more severely, and been exposed to death again and again. Five times I received from the Jews the forty lashes minus one. Three times I was beaten with rods, once I was pelted with stones, three times I was shipwrecked, I spent a night and a day in the open sea, I have been constantly on the move. I have been in danger from rivers, in danger from bandits, in danger from my fellow Jews, in danger from Gentiles; in danger in the city, in danger in the country, in danger at sea; and in danger from false believers. I have labored and toiled and have often gone without sleep; I have known hunger and thirst and have often gone without food; I have been cold and naked. Besides everything else, I face daily the pressure of my concern for all the churches. Who is weak, and I do not feel weak? Who is led into sin, and I do not inwardly burn?
—2 Corinthians 11:23-29

In the Old Testament, we see the same willingness to pay a steep price to honor God. Babylonian King Nebuchadnezzar, like the Roman emperors centuries later, wanted to be worshiped, so he made a statue of gold ninety feet high and called all the administrators of his kingdom to come to worship. The ceremony was elaborate (and loud), but three Hebrew friends—Shadrach, Meshach, and Abednego—refused to participate. Nebuchadnezzar was outraged. He summoned the three men and gave them one last chance to worship the statue. If they refused, he was going to throw them into a furnace to be incinerated. The men responded:

"King Nebuchadnezzar, we do not need to defend ourselves before you in this matter. If we are thrown into the blazing furnace, the God we serve is able to deliver us from it, and he will deliver us from Your Majesty's hand. But even if he does not, we want you to know, Your Majesty, that we will not serve your gods or worship the image of gold you have set up." —Daniel 3:16-18

Either way, they were determined to be faithful to God's will and ways. Nebuchadnezzar commanded his soldiers to throw them into the fire which was so hot that the soldiers died in the flames. But in the furnace, the king saw a fourth man walking with the friends. It was almost certainly a christophany, an appearance of the preincarnate Christ, who saved them.

Another account in Scripture tells of a woman who took a great risk to speak up for God's people who were being oppressed. Esther had been chosen to be the king's wife because of her beauty. When her uncle Mordecai discovered a plot to kill all the Jews, he went to her to request that she ask the king for mercy. She sent word to him that she couldn't do it without risking her life. He responded:

"Do not think that because you are in the king's house you alone of all the Jews will escape. For if you remain silent at this time, relief and deliverance for the Jews will arise from another place, but you and your father's family will perish. And who knows but that you have come to your royal position for such a time as this?" —Esther 3:13-14

Esther mustered the courage to stand up for her people, and the Jews were saved.

At the height of His popularity, Jesus warned His disciples that popularity wouldn't last. A day was coming when they would be ridiculed and persecuted:

> *"I tell you, my friends, do not be afraid of those who kill the body and after that can do no more. But I will show you whom you should fear: Fear him who, after your body has been killed, has authority to throw you into hell. Yes, I tell you, fear him. Are not five sparrows sold for two pennies? Yet not one of them is forgotten by God. Indeed, the very hairs of your head are all numbered. Don't be afraid; you are worth more than many sparrows."* —Luke 12:4-7

We live in the most affluent and comfortable culture the world has ever known, and it's easy for Pastors and their teams to conclude that life should always be pleasant in continual growth and strength. As the Scriptures say, "Pride comes before a fall," and arrogance inevitably leads to a collapse— maybe not soon and maybe not very publicly, but it's certain. Wise leaders have a powerful blend of humility (because they don't know the outcome of their decisions) and confidence (because God will have His way and teach important lessons no matter what happens).

WISE LEADERS have a powerful blend of humility (because they don't know the outcome of their decisions) and confidence (because God will have His way and teach important lessons no matter what happens).

FIVE QUESTIONS

No matter how clear a leader's vision may be, it's important to involve others in the process of discovery, planning, and implementation. Over the years, I've learned to ask five crucial questions:

What should we *start*?

I ask, "If we could start any program, any campaign, any outreach, or any other initiative, what would we do? I'm not talking about reframing and reorienting something we're already doing. I'm talking about doing something we've never done before. We're not going to evaluate the ideas, and we're not going to make any decisions. Let your mind wander in places it may never have been before." This is "blue sky thinking," and I welcome any and all ideas. This isn't the time to scrutinize them. Analysis begun too early is often a wet blanket that smothers creativity.

This is a question for churches that are growing and need to find ways to grow even more.

What should we *stop*?

All churches need to figure out what to stop. Something isn't working, so this discussion is designed to identify the roadblocks. It's an open secret what and who isn't effective any longer. Almost certainly, some people in leadership have a deep emotional commitment to programs and events that aren't effective any longer, so don't be surprised when they resist any hint that what they cherish is in jeopardy. In fact, this might not be a group discussion. Ask them to give their input individually. Their feedback might surprise you—or maybe not!

What should we *sustain?*

The right answer to this question isn't "Everything!" All churches need to ask this question because, at least from my experience, if a church has ten programs, three or four of them are exceptionally effective, three or four are moderately effective, and a few continue only because no one has asked the hard questions about their efficacy. This question helps identify what you're continually committed to.

What should we *suspend?*

Some activities and modes of communication have been effective for a while, and they'll probably be again, but for a while, they need to be suspended. Perhaps the best example is when many churches suspended their in-person services during the Delta and Omicron waves of the COVID-19 pandemic. They went online, and they found other ways to connect with their people, but for a while, they didn't meet together in the same room. Similarly, many churches suspend small groups over the summer months when people are traveling.

What should we *speed up?*

When a team identifies the three or four programs that are producing the biggest gains, they should devote more resources to make them even more effective. They can realign priorities and responsibilities, increase the level of communication about these efforts, and do whatever it takes to add higher octane fuel to these engines.

These questions provide a roadmap for a team's journey. When I ask them, I'm not looking for a quick answer, so we can move on to something more important. The discussion itself is important, and I want to involve everyone in the discussion. Many times, people who have been quiet have brilliant insights that no one has asked them to share before.

WHEN I ask questions, I'm not looking for a quick answer, so we can move on to something more important. The discussion itself is important, and I want to involve everyone in the discussion.

EI

In his insightful book *Emotional Intelligence*, Daniel Goleman describes the necessity for people, especially leaders, to manage feelings, so they are expressed appropriately. This trait, he asserts, is "the largest single predictor of success"[23] in any career. Throughout this book, I'm making the assumption that leaders are growing in every aspect of their lives, including their emotional maturity. We know the gospel speaks what our hearts long to hear: we're so sinful that it took the death of the Son of God to pay for our sins, but He loves us so much that He was glad to die for us. We're deeply loved, fully forgiven, and completely accepted in Christ. In fact, the Father loves us as much as He loves Jesus, and Jesus loves us as much as the Father loves Him!

You can't get any more secure than that. But we're thoroughly human, and though we've taught these truths for

---

23 Daniel Goleman, *Emotional Intelligence* (New York: Bantam Books, 2006).

years, sometimes they haven't penetrated into the depths of our souls. Goleman observes:

> Cognitive skills such as big-picture thinking and long-term vision were particularly important. But when I calculated the ratio of technical skills, IQ, and emotional intelligence as ingredients of excellent performance, emotional intelligence proved to be twice as important as the others for jobs at all levels. . . . If your emotional abilities aren't in hand, if you don't have self-awareness, if you are not able to manage your distressing emotions, if you can't have empathy and have effective relationships, then no matter how smart you are, you are not going to get very far.[24]

Let me ask: When was the last time you got upset? Was it proportionate to the event, or was it too much or too little? If you observed someone respond as you did, would you think it was good, right, and appropriate?

If you're leading your church into and through chaos, you can be sure that tensions will rise, frustrations will mount, and suspicions will threaten to erode trust. Even if others around you are coming unglued, you need the self-awareness to see the rising emotions and the ability to manage them. If you can't do that, you may manipulate people, and you may intimidate them, but you won't really be able to lead them because they won't follow someone they don't respect.

Let me go back to the story about Dave and his church. At every stage, he was well aware of the possibilities and pitfalls: at the entrepreneurial inception of his vision, as it emerged in actual programs and job descriptions, and as it changed the culture. Then, when he noticed the fork in the road, he saw

---

24 Daniel Goleman, *The Emotionally Intelligent Leader* (Cambridge, MA: Harvard Business Review, 2020), audiobook.

the possibilities and pitfalls of being enterprising, as well as the pitfalls and benefits of not rocking the boat when things were going well. But Dave didn't just see these things; he involved his Board and team in substantive, beneficial discussions about all he anticipated. At each point, his people were informed, they felt heard and understood, and he gave them time to adjust to changes in reporting and responsibilities. For a young man, his emotional maturity was (and still is) remarkable.

We've addressed the importance of a leader's communication with the Board and Leadership Team, but we've only mentioned another vital audience: influencers. Every church has them. They may not have a formal title or role, but people look to them as sources of insight. They hold court in the lobby before and after services, in the coffee shop, and wherever others can draw on their observations. A Pastor may do a fantastic job communicating with a Board and Leadership Team but be blindsided by influencers who weren't brought into the conversation. You know who they are. They're the ones people talk about when they say, "Well, she told me..." or "That's not what he said." If your influencers aren't supportive, you can expect rough seas ahead for any new vision.

PASTORS need to encourage people to
support the vision more than the visionary.

In addition, Pastors need to encourage people to support the vision more than the visionary. I've heard Board members, team members, and influencers say something like, "Well, I'm not too sure about the Pastor's new idea, but I like him and I support him." Loyalty to the person is good, but it's not good enough! If people are primarily loyal to the Pastor, they're *for* him, but if they embrace the vision, they're together *with* him in the effort. There's a big difference. Their *why* needs to be much bigger than their relationship with the Pastor. It may start there, but it shouldn't end there.

Personal loyalty makes insecure leaders feel better about themselves, but if they have an ounce of discernment, they know it's fickle and fleeting. They have to keep pleasing the person to retain loyalty. But if they're together in their goal of fulfilling a bigger vision, they don't have to play games at pleasing each other, hiding how they really feel and think, or proving themselves again and again. A common why, a shared purpose, is both powerful and sustainable.

Pastors simply can't avoid chaos, but they can choose what kind they experience. If they move forward with a bold vision, they create the kind of unease I've described in this book. However, if they're timid and passive, they create a very different kind of chaos, the kind when people feel frustrated— they want to be inspired and led, but the Pastor isn't doing or can't do it. They grumble, they gossip, they complain, and the Pastor responds defensively. That's not the kind of chaos any of us want to endure!

Dave created chaos at his church, but it was carefully orchestrated chaos. His bold vision for community outreach and then a residency church-planting arm shook up his church, and it had a remarkable impact on his people, his city, and many other churches. The residency program isn't all they're doing: Their job training program has equipped over two hundred people by helping them find meaningful, good-paying work in their city. The church's Christian school welcomes students from disadvantaged parts of town, and a food pantry provides nourishment for those who can't afford it and those who don't have transportation to a grocery store. To date, more than two dozen churches have been planted in America and forty overseas, and the church planters follow Dave's example of creating programs that make a difference in their communities.

Dave's influence goes far beyond the walls of his church. Other Pastors look to him for ideas and inspiration . . . and in him, they find an abundance of both.

By perseverance the snail reached the ark.
—Charles Spurgeon

CONSIDER THIS:

1) Whom do you know who is a good example of an entrepreneurial Pastor or church leader? What impact does that person have on others, especially you?
2) How would you describe the transition of the stages from entrepreneurial to emerging and from emerging to established? What has to happen?
3) What are the possibilities and pitfalls leaders have to face each time?
4) How have you seen these stages in a church's life? Describe how the transitions were handled.
5) What are some signs a church is facing a choice between erosion and enterprising in a fresh way?
6) Do you see any of those signs in your church?
7) How would asking (and answering) the five questions help you and your team?
8) Spend some time reflecting on the five questions and discussing them with the Board and team.
9) Why do you think emotional intelligence is more important than skills and raw intelligence? What are some steps you can take to raise your level of EQ?

CHAPTER 8

NOW AND LATER

Indignation and compassion form a powerful combination.
They are indispensable to vision, and therefore to leadership.

—John Stott

W hen I share the concepts in this book with Pastors and other church leaders, many of them intuitively grasp the implications, and virtually all of them ask a version of this question: "Sam, this is really helpful. What can I do now to prepare my people for chaos?"

WHAT CAN I do now to prepare my people for chaos?

I introduced the idea of "the muddy middle" earlier in the book. It's one of the most important concepts for leaders and their teams to understand. In any new venture, leaders can expect two gaps: one between the initial casting of the vision and the first steps of implementation and another between the first steps and the fulfillment of the dream. These two periods may last weeks, or they may last months . . . and occasionally, even years. They are times the leader and the vision are most at risk because people are confused and frustrated that so much work has produced such little results.

I encourage leaders to understand that these periods, which I call "the muddy middle," always happen, so they shouldn't be surprised. If they anticipate them, these seemingly dry seasons can build trust instead of eroding it and revitalize people instead of causing them to become passive. They are plateaus for people to regroup, reassess the process, and reaffirm the reason they began in the first place. In these times, conflict often rises with the frustration level, so it's a good time for leaders to affirm people in their roles, validate the range of emotions, and help people nip resentment in the bud.

Things that are worthwhile don't come easily. They come at a cost, but the best leaders capitalize on the strain of reaching higher by forming even stronger bonds of respect and cooperation. In this sense, leaders need to wear bifocals, keeping an eye on the ultimate goal while shepherding the interactions of the team very closely.

DO THIS, NOT THAT

Over the past few decades, I've had the privilege of observing some of the finest leaders in the world as they trusted God and mobilized people to do something greater than they ever imagined. These leaders remained lions about their grand and sweeping goals, and they inspired their people every step of the way. These are the traits and decisions I've seen in them:

1) **Understand yourself.**

Be a student of your gifts and strengths, and be honest about the holes in your leadership—and all of us have them. Self-leadership is crucial. Leaders who are self-aware help their people be observant about their own strengths and deficiencies, too. When we know what we do well, we can maximize those talents, and when we know where we often fall short, we can find ways to compensate by employing other resources. One of the main complaints I hear from team members is that they don't believe their Pastor sees his own weaknesses. Leaders who aren't aware and honest about them often try to be a Superman or Wonder Woman. It's a role they weren't meant to play.

Pastor and author Paul David Tripp encourages us, "Remember, it is not your weakness that will get in the way of God's working through you, but your delusions of strength. His strength is made perfect in our weakness! Point to His strength by being willing to admit your weakness."

2) **Value others.**

A leader who feels comfortable with an honest self-assessment doesn't need to wear a mask of competence; instead, that person creates an environment where mutual affirmation brings out the best in everyone. Transactional leaders focus on the tasks and use people to accomplish them (and people usually *feel* used). Relational leaders realize their people are their greatest assets, and if they thrive, the goals will probably be met and exceeded.

3) **Value questions.**

One of the most obvious marks of leadership is the response to questions. Good leaders invite people to ask questions, even and especially those that challenge the leaders' views. These leaders don't react defensively. They engage, ask for clarification, and value the process of discovery. Poor leaders see questions as an attack on their authority, and they feel threatened. They always have to be right, and they have to be seen as having all the answers.

4) Cultivate patience.

By definition, leaders are going somewhere and taking people with them, but their people need them to be patient as they try to understand the big picture and their role in accomplishing it. I marvel at Jesus' patience with the disciples. He taught them and modeled life in the kingdom of God, but they were slow on the uptake. Occasionally, He had to warn them or reprove them, but it appears He said far less than we might have! Patience is more than time. It's an attitude of, *I want you to succeed, and I'll do whatever I can for as long as it takes, so you can grasp your role and thrive in it.* Leaders who don't demonstrate patience are inherently anxious and demanding, creating unhealthy tension instead of gently calling out the best in each person. They create a whiplash of expectations: Insecure leaders are happy when things are humming along, but when things aren't going well or fast enough, they march in with a new plan, often communicated with an air of contempt for those who aren't contributing as much as the leader expected. Patience is associated with empathy, putting ourselves in the place of others, feeling what they feel, and hoping what they hope.

5) Teach continually.

Every vision has many layers of meaning, and it's important for leaders to communicate the why as well as the who, what, when, where, how, and how much. In fact, many team members quickly gravitate to the tactical issues, so leaders need to continually point them to the bigger picture. Jesus was a master storyteller. He taught by giving people mental images of life in the kingdom. As we teach our people, they need more than concepts; they need stories that capture their hearts.

6) **Validate the sense of loss.**

All change is about loss—the loss of familiarity, the loss of comfort, and the loss of stability. When leaders demonstrate that they understand the price their people will pay, they build trust. When they demand that people "just get over" their sense of discomfort with change, they create a barrier between them and their people. When loss is validated, people can grieve and find new footing; when it isn't, they intuitively believe the leader doesn't understand them and doesn't really care for them. The grieving process doesn't need to take forever, but it does take some time. This doesn't mean the person is out of the game when he's grieving; it means he needs a measure of empathy during the period of adjustment.

WHEN LOSS is validated, people can grieve and find new footing.... The grieving process doesn't need to take forever, but it does take some time.

---

7) **Create a hope-filled language.**

I encourage leaders to step away from themselves and observe what they say to their Boards and their teams. What's the message they're really communicating? Is it one full of hope and enthusiasm, or is it thinly veiled disappointment and resentment? I heard about a Pastor whose often-repeated rhetorical refrain was, "One more trip around the wilderness," an obvious allusion to the children of Israel spending forty years in the desert. His Board members knew he was condemning them and the church for some unidentified disobedience which the Pastor assumed was the reason the church wasn't growing.

We need to use language that gives people a sense that the process may be hard, but it's worth it. "We're running a marathon, and we're approaching the steepest part of the climb. We'll run together. No one will be left behind." "We can do this. Emmanuel is with us!" "We have nothing to prove, except to make God proud of us." "Our goals are our goals. No one is imposing them on us. Let's trust God and see what happens." "We're on a journey together. Let's enjoy the ride. It's up to all of us to make sure we don't run into a ditch on one side or the other!"

8) **Develop a culture of gratitude.**

Leaders carry a heavy burden, but too many of them show it on their faces! Those who cultivate a positive atmosphere instill confidence in their Board and team. When they see the leader's optimism, they find rays of light even in the darkest times. And when they sense a leader's bedrock of gratitude, they look for silver linings, too. Gratitude is both a word and a theme: a simple "Thank you" or "You're really good at that" can be spoken in an instant, and a mature, secure leader can always find reasons to thank God. The Psalms are brutally honest expressions of the full range of emotions. Half of them are what one scholar called "wintry," but the last five are pure praise and thanksgiving.

In his book *Answering God,* Pastor and author Eugene Peterson scans the Psalms and observes that the last five are the ultimate end of them all:

All prayer, pursued far enough, becomes praise. Any prayer, no matter how desperate its origin, no matter how angry and fearful the experiences it traverses, ends up in praise. It does not always get there quickly or easily—the trip can take a lifetime—but the end is always praise. 'Praises,' in fact, is the only accurate title for our prayer book, for it is the goal that shapes the journey: 'The end is where we start from.'"[25]

I believe there is an inverse relationship between arrogance and gratitude: arrogant leaders aren't grateful, and grateful leaders aren't arrogant.

9) **Look often in the rearview mirror.**

Realize that you're the product of people who have poured themselves into your life and your ministry. No one comes into the room on their own. All of us were brought to our role as leaders. You stand on the shoulders of others, and your greatest impact for the kingdom is to let people stand on your shoulders.

So, what can leaders do now to prepare themselves and their teams for a new season of growth? My answer is that they can do a rigorous assessment of these nine traits and behaviors. Will they need to make some adjustments? Undoubtedly. Will they have the courage? We'll see.

---

25 Eugene Peterson, *Answering God* (San Francisco: HarperOne, 1991), 121-128.

ALWAYS A LION

As I mentioned, I love to watch shows about nature preserves in Africa, and I'm always fascinated by the behavior of lions. They're not called "the king of beasts" for nothing. The eye of every gazelle, every chimp, every wildebeest, every warthog, every buffalo, every elephant, and every bird are on them. Where are they? What are they doing? What havoc will they create next? I believe this is the nature of true leadership. Yes, I know that this metaphor has limitations. I'm not advocating that you become a ferocious predator! But I'm certainly pushing you to be bold and assertive, to make waves, to create chaos…in ways that are supportive, productive, meaningful, kind, and honoring to God.

DON'T DRIFT into being a house cat, and if you think you are one, get an infusion of lion DNA and roar again!

Don't drift into being a house cat, and if you think you are one, get an infusion of lion DNA and roar again! The heroes of the faith in Hebrews 11 didn't get up in the morning and say, "I think I'll be tame today. I plan to blend into the background and avoid making waves. That's good enough for me, and it's good enough for God." No, they were determined to make a difference, and they were willing to pay any price to make it happen.

Caleb was one of the twelve spies sent by Moses into the Promised Land to give a report about the strength of the enemy there. When they returned, ten of them said the enemy was too strong for them, and they recommended backing away from the risk. But Caleb and Joshua gave the minority report, full of hope and courage. Moses took the advice of the ten, and the people of God wandered for forty years—long enough for all of those who had been slaves to die on the journey . . . all except for Caleb and Joshua. During those decades, I'm sure their hearts burned for the opportunity to cross the Jordan and enter the land, and finally, they got their chance. Joshua became the designated leader and military general. As the people spread throughout the land and conquered the people that lived there, Joshua assigned territory to each of the twelve tribes of Israel. For five years, the battles raged. Then, Caleb said to Joshua,

> "You know what the Lord said to Moses the man of God at Kadesh Barnea about you and me. I was forty years old when Moses the servant of the Lord sent me from Kadesh Barnea to explore the land. And I brought him back a report according to my convictions, but my fellow Israelites who went up with me made the hearts of the people melt in fear. I, however, followed the Lord my God wholeheartedly. So on that day Moses swore to me, 'The land on which your feet have walked will be your inheritance and that of your children forever, because you have followed the Lord my God wholeheartedly.'"

Then, Caleb showed that even as an old man, he was still a lion:

> "Now then, just as the Lord promised, he has kept me alive for forty-five years since the time he said this to Moses, while Israel moved about in the wilderness. So here I am today, eighty-five years old! I am still as strong today as

*the day Moses sent me out; I'm just as vigorous to go out to
battle now as I was then. Now give me this hill country that
the Lord promised me that day. You yourself heard then
that the Anakites were there and their cities were large and
fortified, but, the Lord helping me, I will drive them out just
as he said."* —Joshua 14:6-12

"Give me this hill country." That's not the fertile plains;
it's the region of Judah with rolling hills and rocky outcrop-
pings. Caleb wasn't asking for the easy, comfortable part of the
country. He was calling the promise due, but Joshua didn't have
the ability to simply give the land to Caleb. The old man fought
for it and won it. The promise was entirely God's offer, but the
acquisition required the courage and skill of a mature lion.

What's the hill country for you? What promise has God
spoken to your heart that remains unfulfilled and uncon-
quered? Has it been a long time since a promise burned in your
soul, and you couldn't stop daydreaming about it? Or is it still
fresh? Even if you're old, don't give up on God's promises. Keep
believing, keep fighting, and keep pressing toward God's best.

DON'T GIVE up on God's promises. Keep believing,
keep fighting, and keep pressing toward God's best.

Young lions roar loudly, but they often need to be more
selective about their pursuits. The vision may not have crys-
tallized yet, so they launch into several directions, one after
the other. Still, those around them feel inspired by their zeal.

Older lions roar, and their pursuits have been tailored by time. They know themselves, they have a track record of relational leadership, their vision is clear, and they've been on the journey long enough to be patient with the process.

Never stop being a lion.

CONSIDER THIS:

1) How would you define and describe "the muddy middle"? What are some problems that can occur when leaders don't help their teams navigate those gaps?

2) On a scale of 0 (not in the least) to 10 (Olympic!), evaluate how well you exemplify the traits of good leadership in this chapter:

- Understand yourself _____
- Value others _____
- Value questions _____
- Cultivate patience _____
- Teach continually _____
- Validate the sense of loss _____
- Create a hope-filled language _____
- Develop a culture of gratitude _____
- Look often in the rearview mirror _____

3) In which of these do you excel? How can you maximize these traits?

4) Which ones need some attention? What are some steps you can take in the next week to at least begin to improve in these areas?

5) Do you see yourself as a lion? Why or why not?

6) What are two or three of the most important lessons you've learned from this book?

AVAIL +

FOLLOW
THE
LEADER

STAY CONNECTED

 facebook.com/TheArtofAvail   @theartofavail

AVAIL

AVAIL
PODCAST

THE AVAIL PODCAST

HOSTED BY VIRGIL SIERRA

CPSIA information can be obtained
at www.ICGtesting.com
Printed in the USA
BVHW051113231222
654916BV00016B/754